where will this train take me

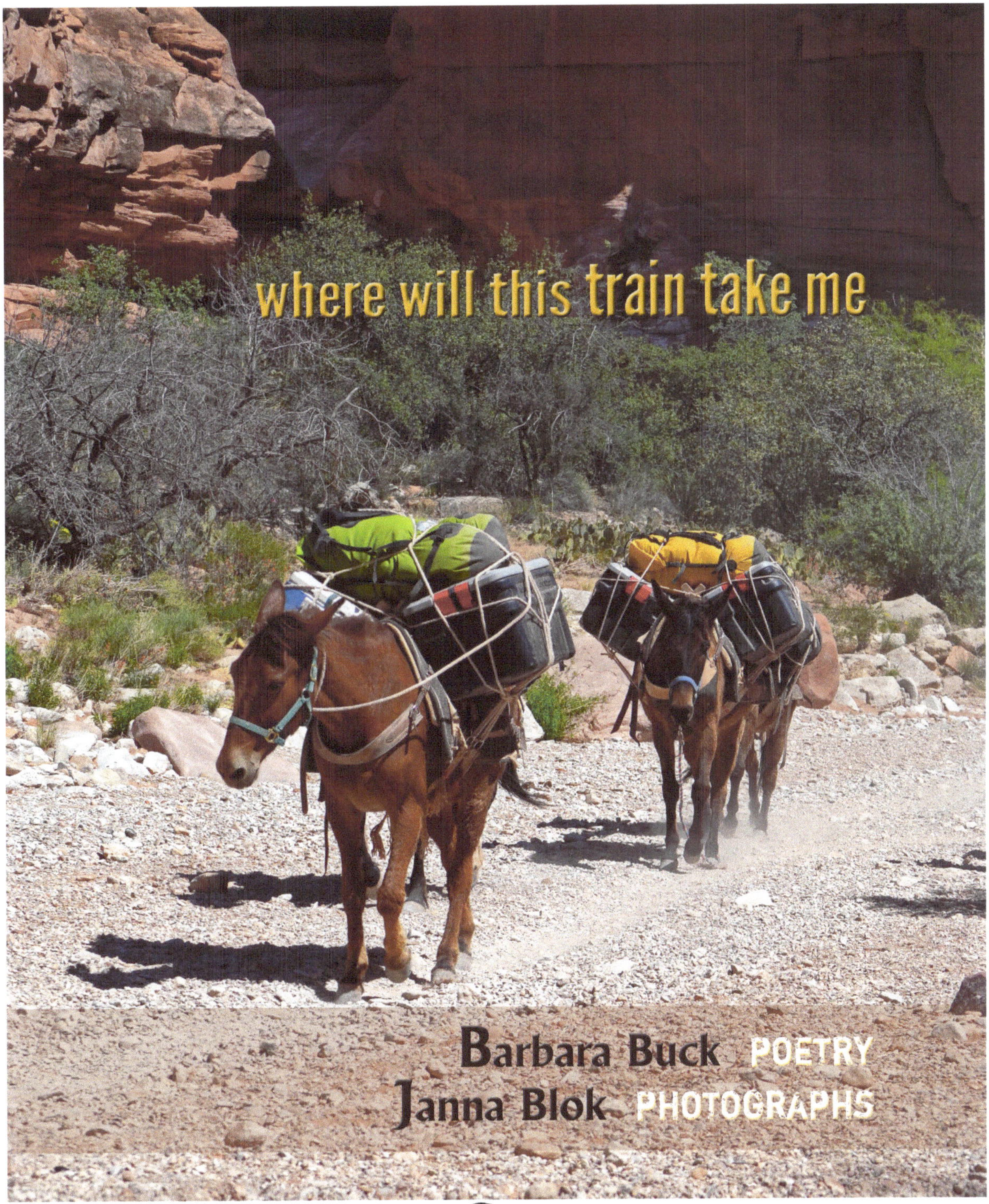

where will this train take me

Barbara Buck POETRY
Janna Blok PHOTOGRAPHS

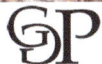

GusGus Press • Bedazzled Ink Publishing
Fairfield, California

© 2017 Barbara Buck
© 2017 Janna Blok

All rights reserved. No part of this publication may be reproduced or
transmitted in any means,
electronic or mechanical, without permission in
writing from the publisher.

978-1-945805-60-8 paperback

Cover Design
by

Typeset
by
WolFyre Press
Studio

GusGus Press
a division of
Bedazzled Ink Publishing Company
Fairfield, California
http://gusgus.bedazzledink.com

Dedicated To Our Respective Children and To Their Children.

We also thank our friend, Glenda Jones, very much for her hours spent putting our material into an acceptable digital format for publication.

junior high
batting her lashes
snapping her gum

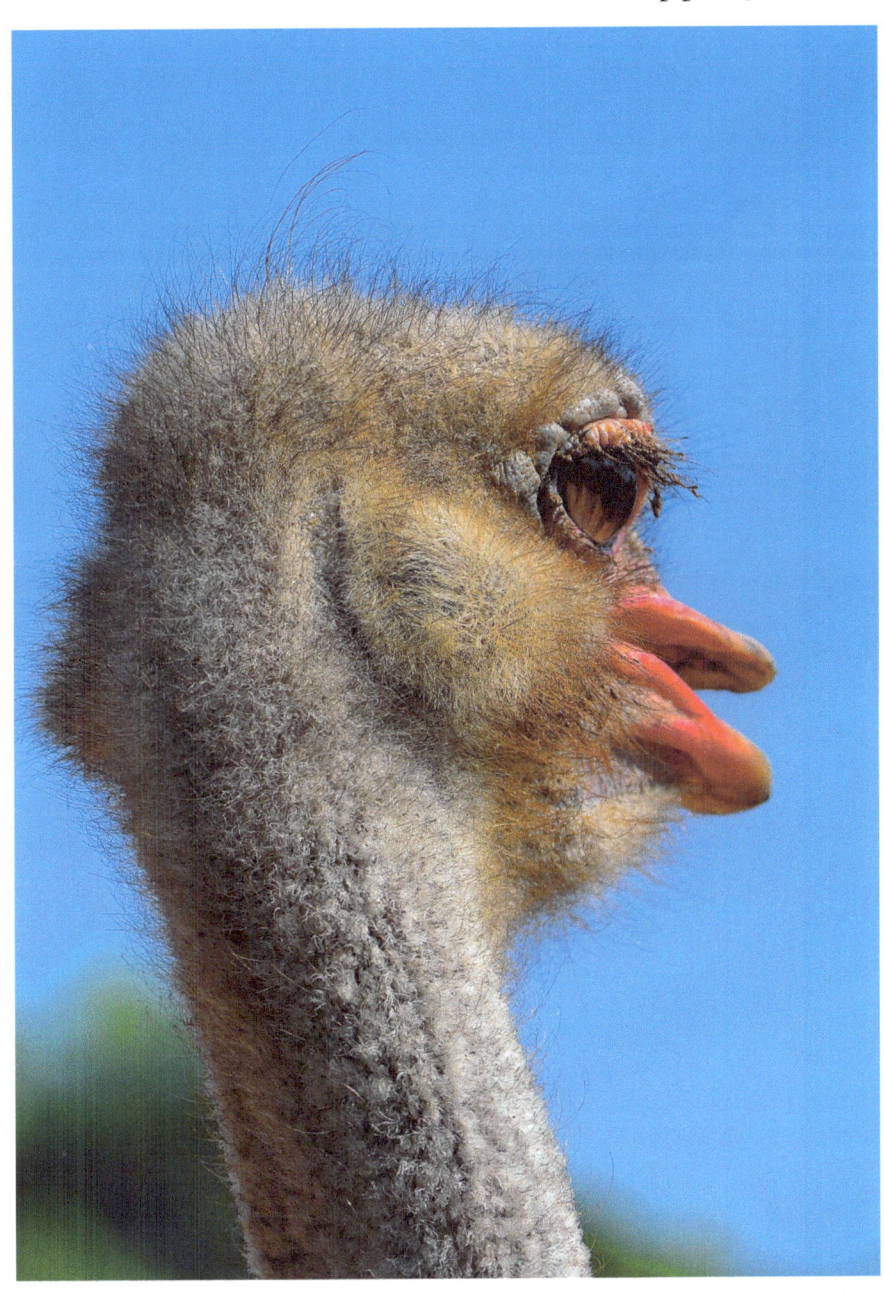

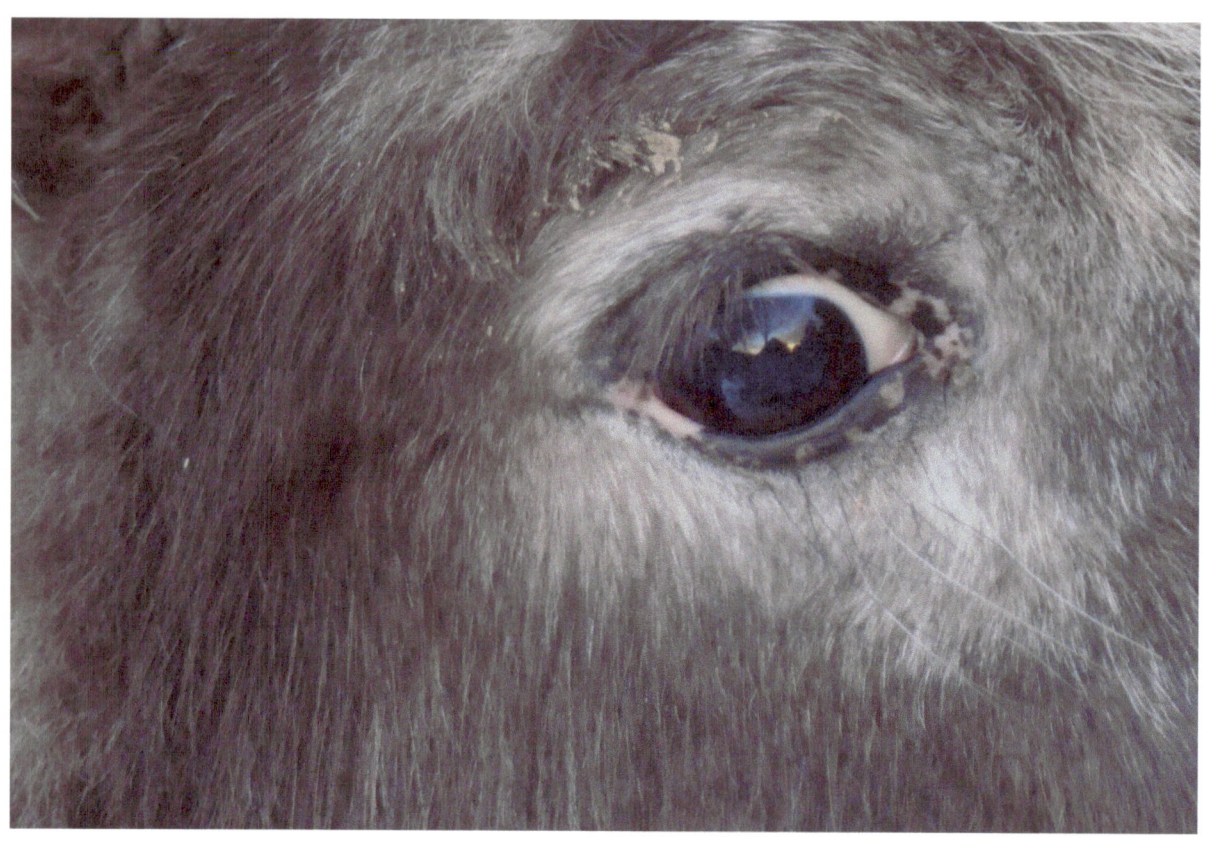

eye
reflection
see

next meal
carry in
waiting

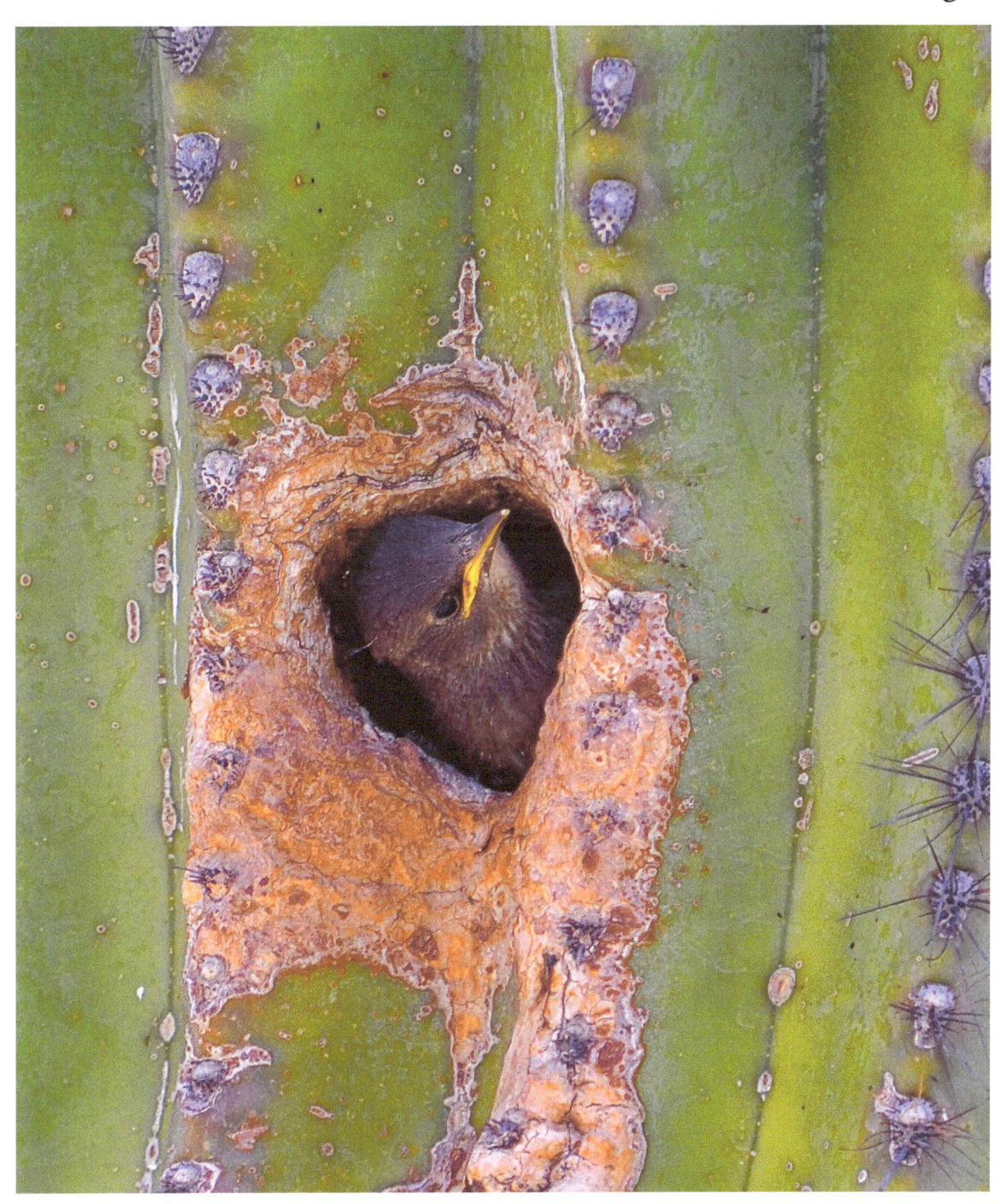

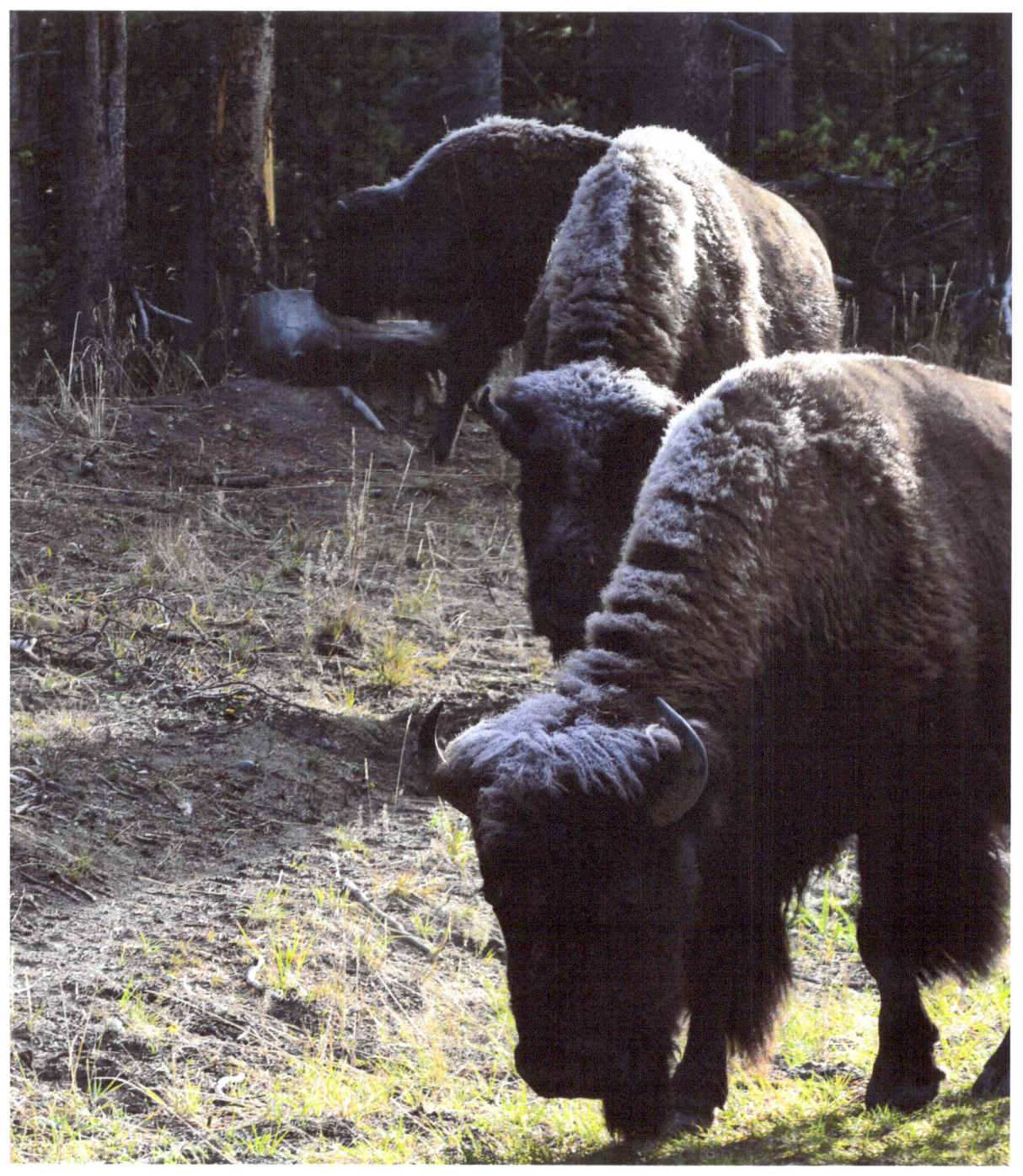

nature
America
gift

wireless
wilderness

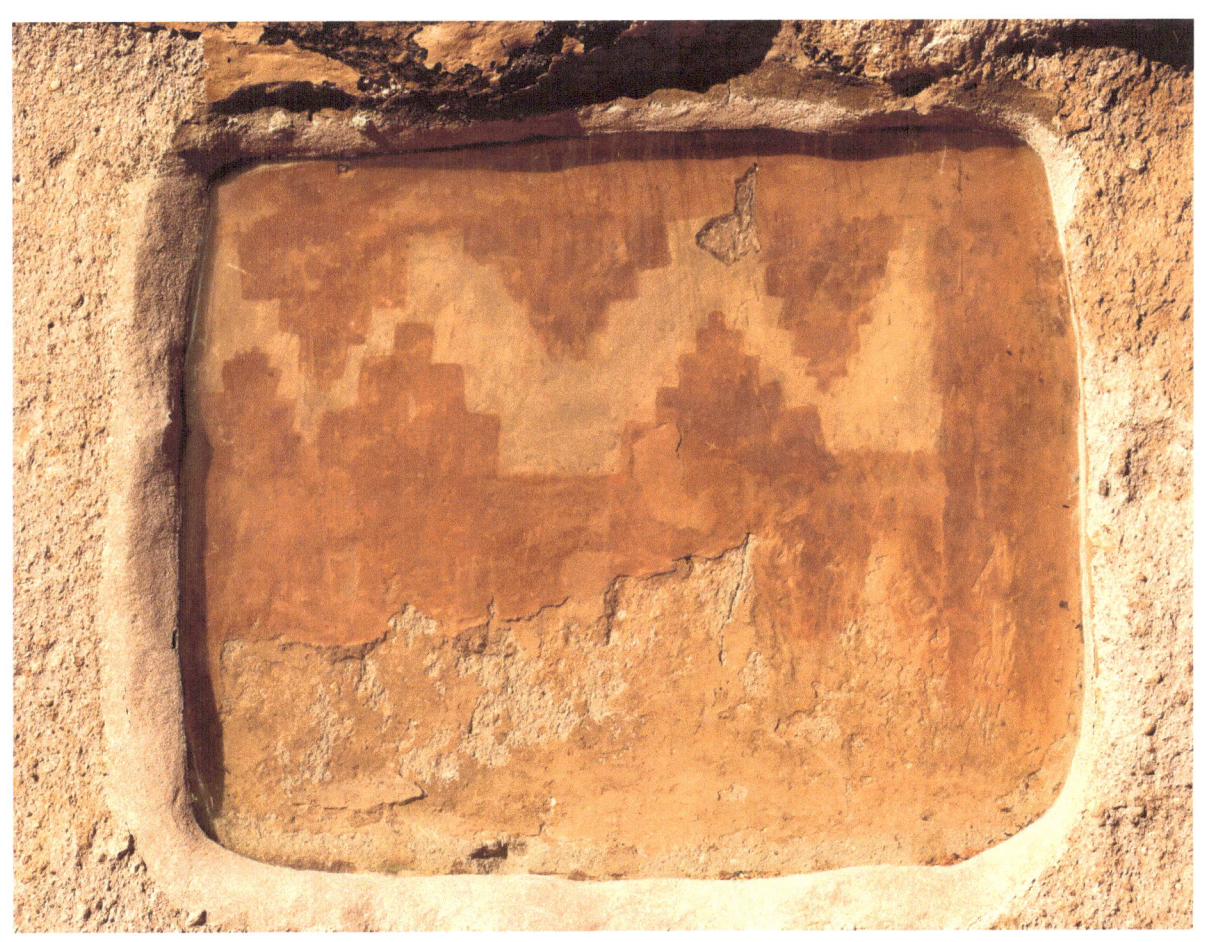

youngsters
upscale
content for now

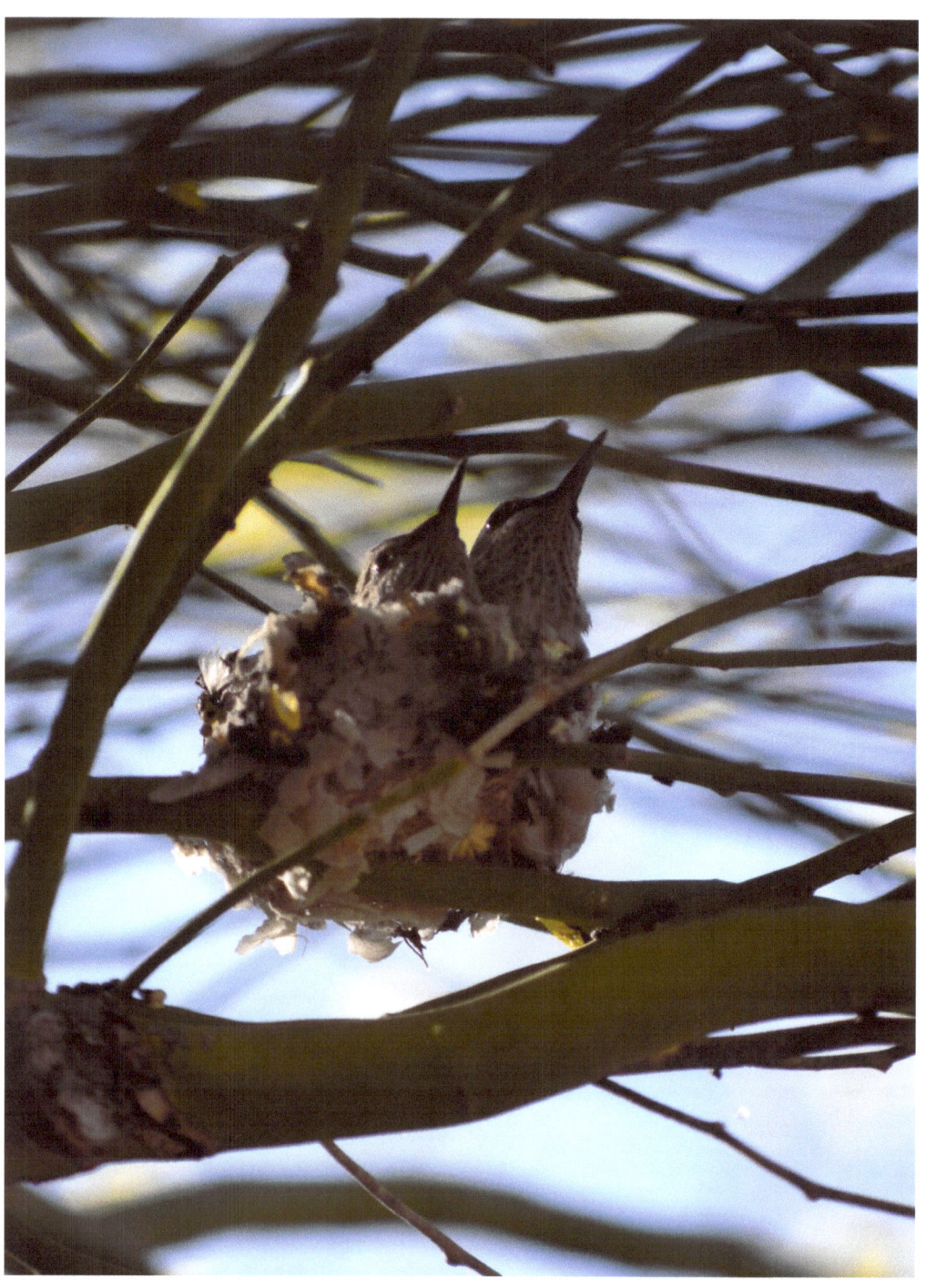

extending
light
energy

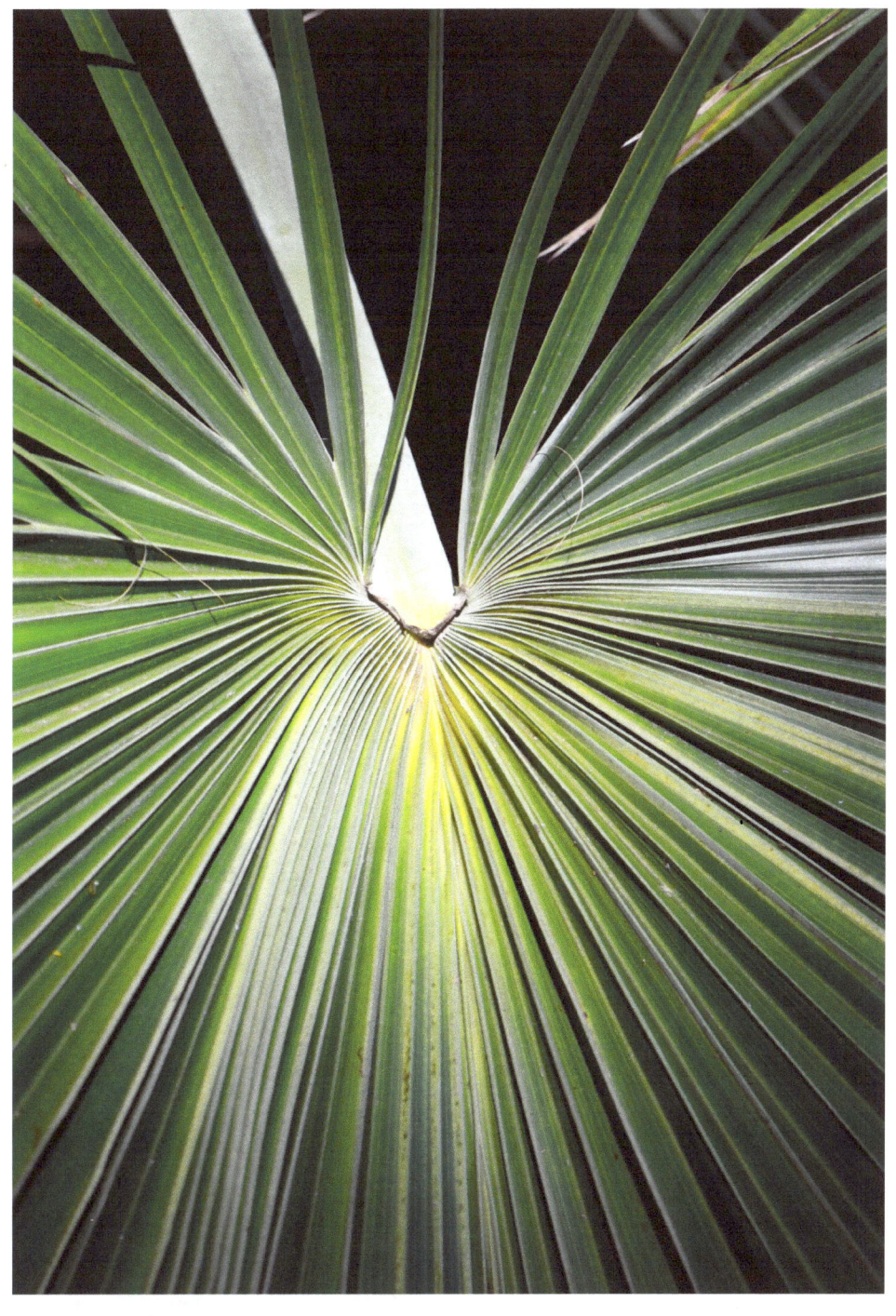

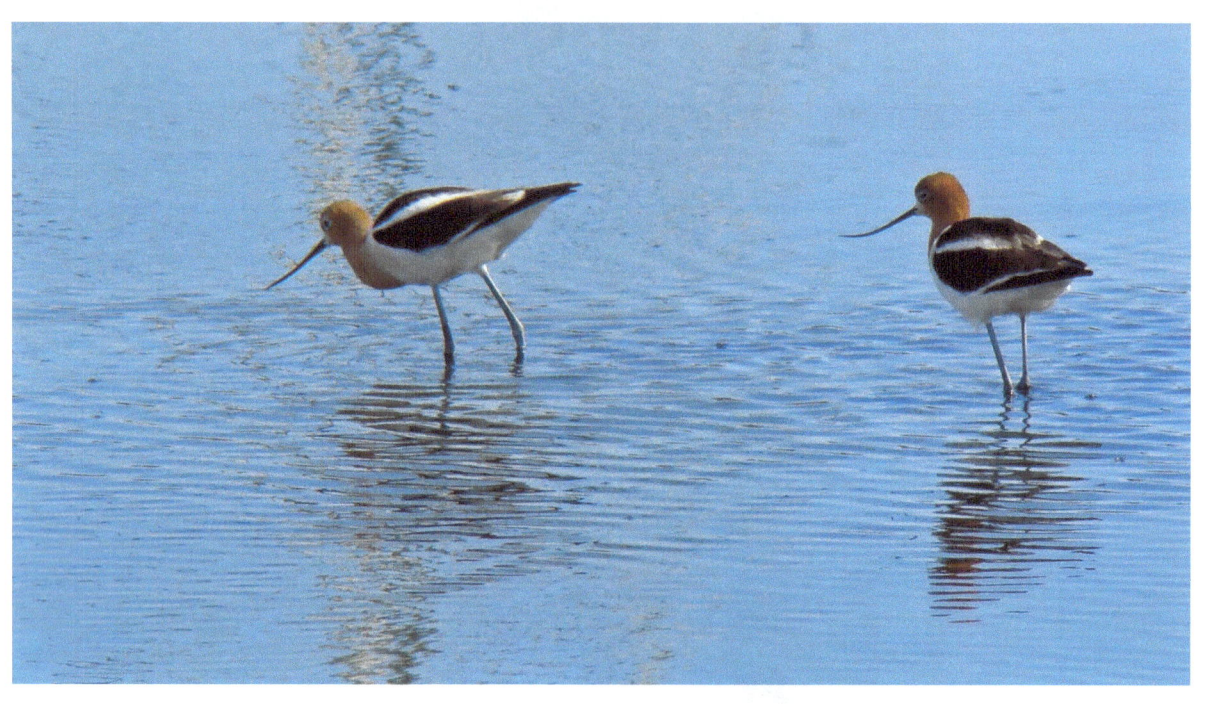

springtime
hormones
adults

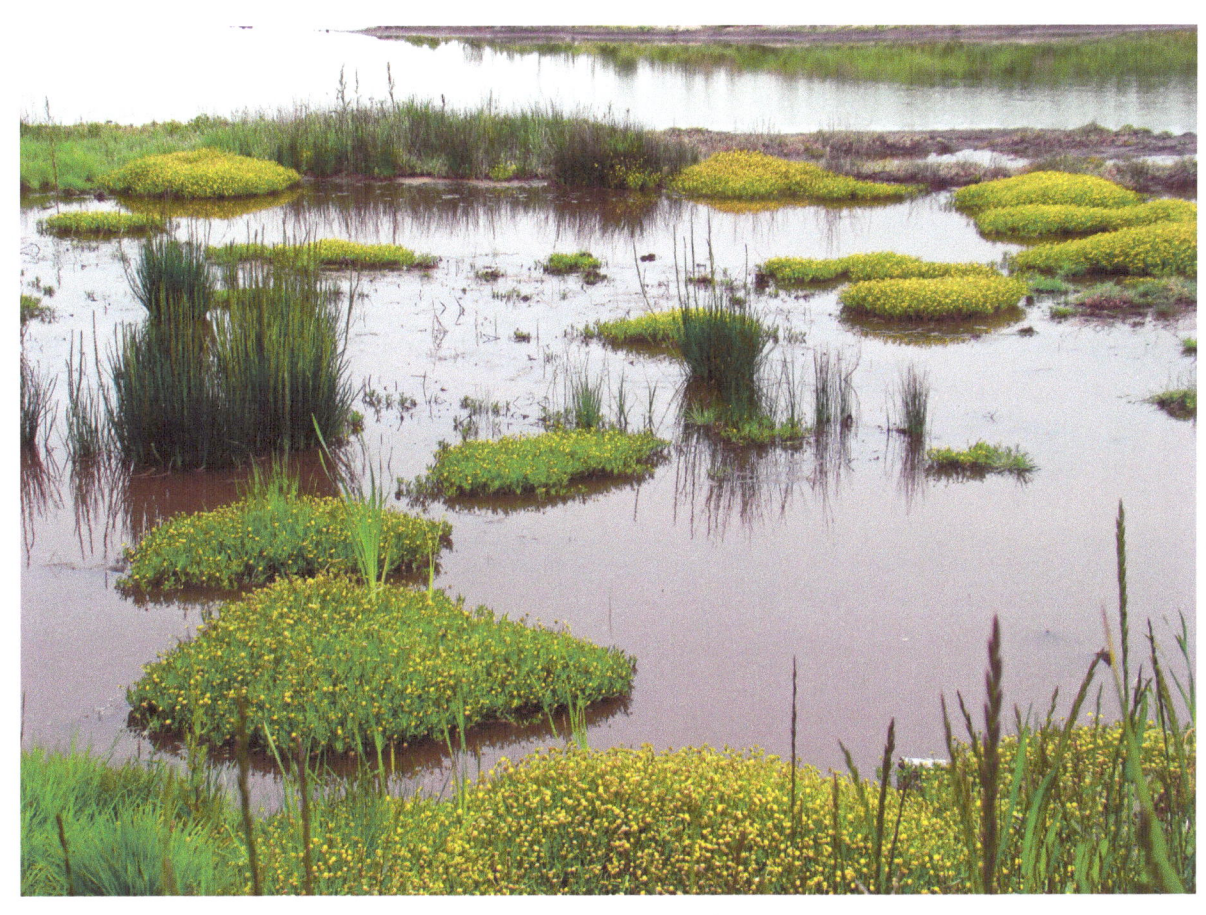

barrier
mainland
in bloom

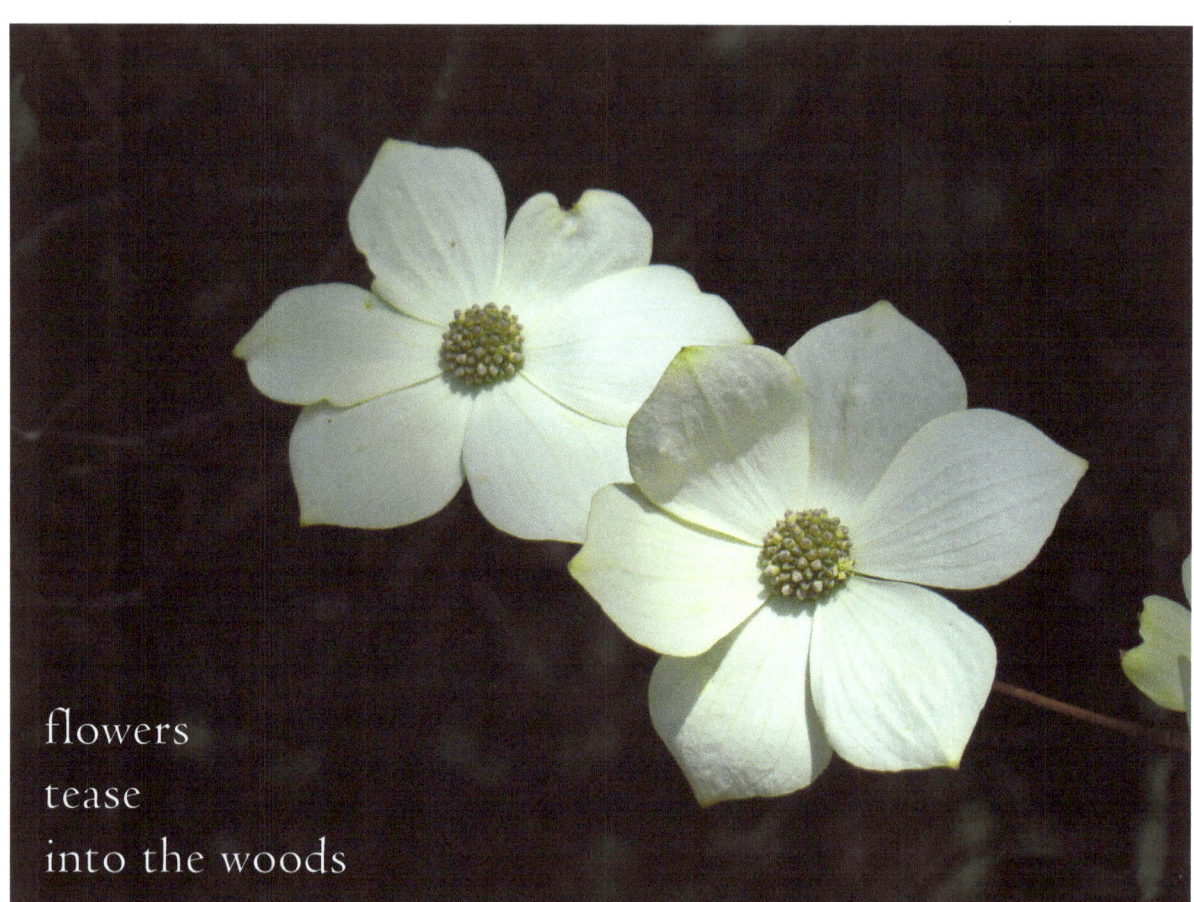

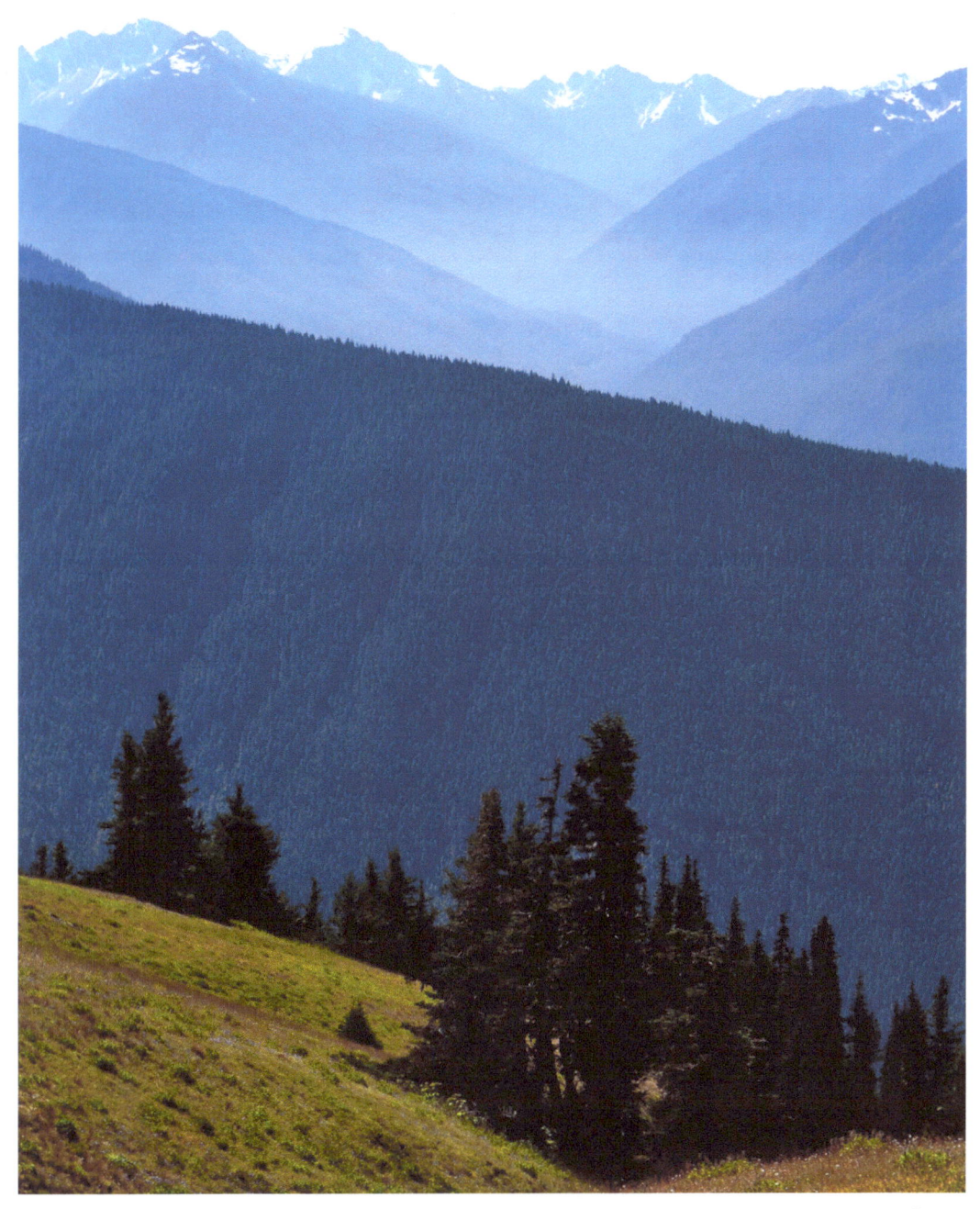

future
in the
foreground

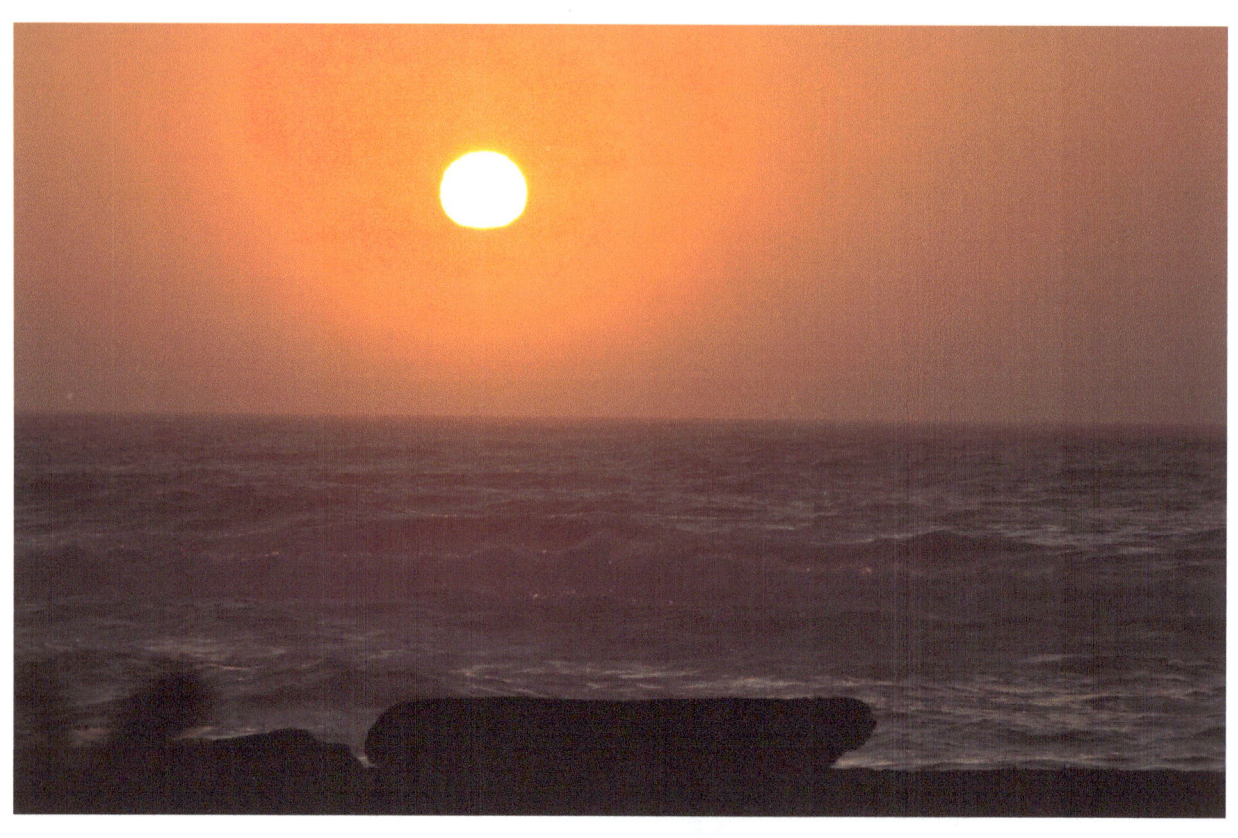

glowing
horizon
peacefully

discordant pathways
gyroscope
civil discourse

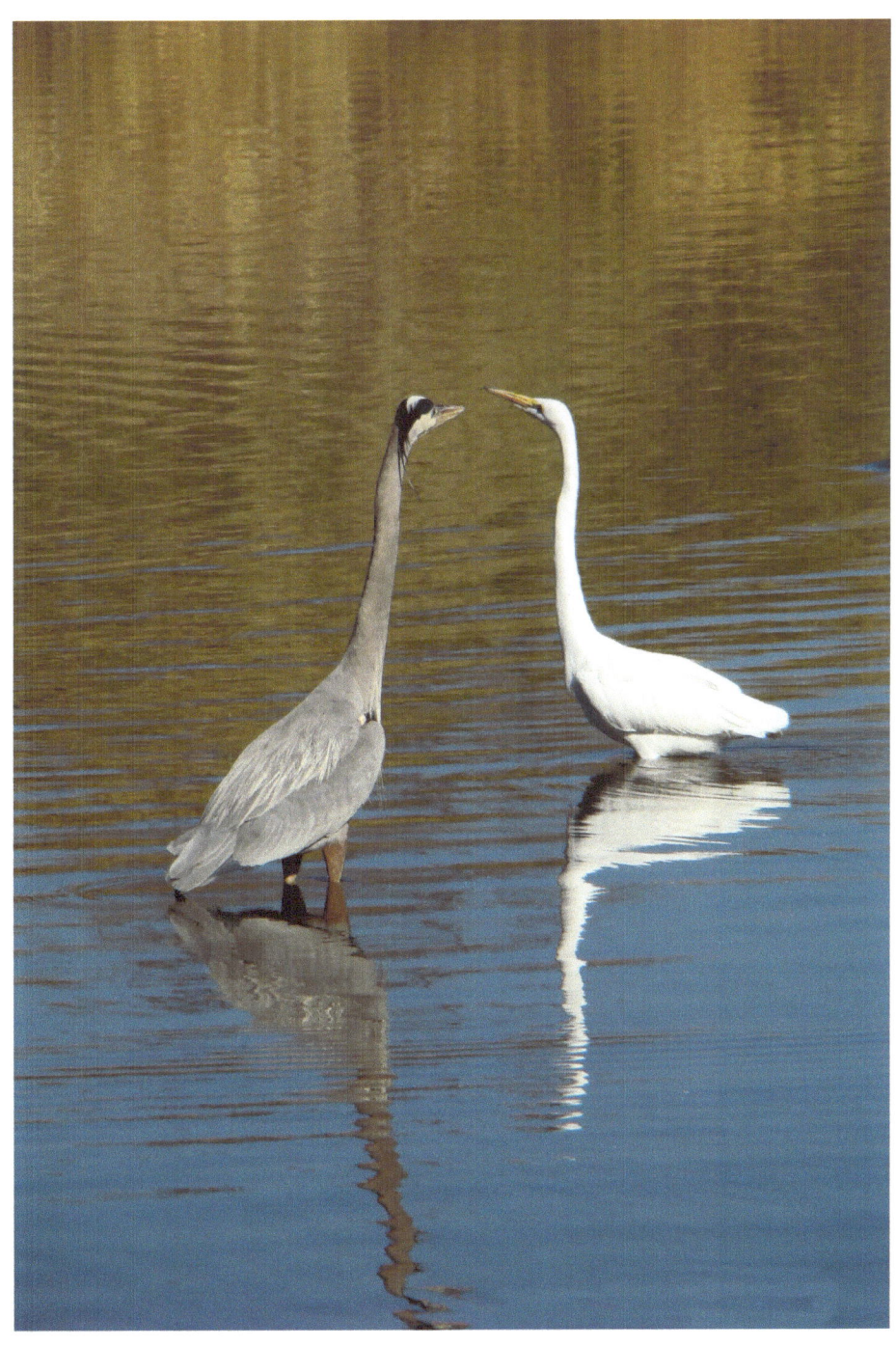

grace
snapping turtle
under pressure

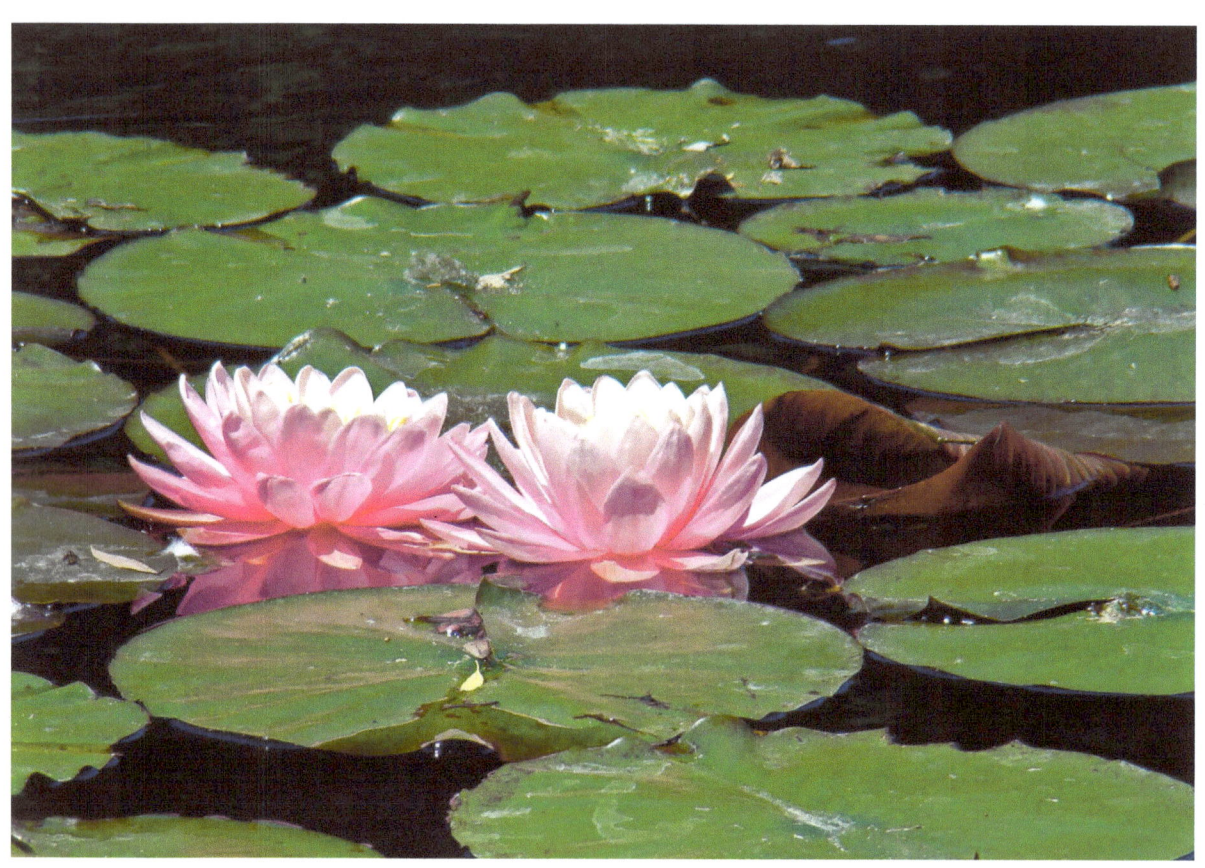

distant
focus
reaches

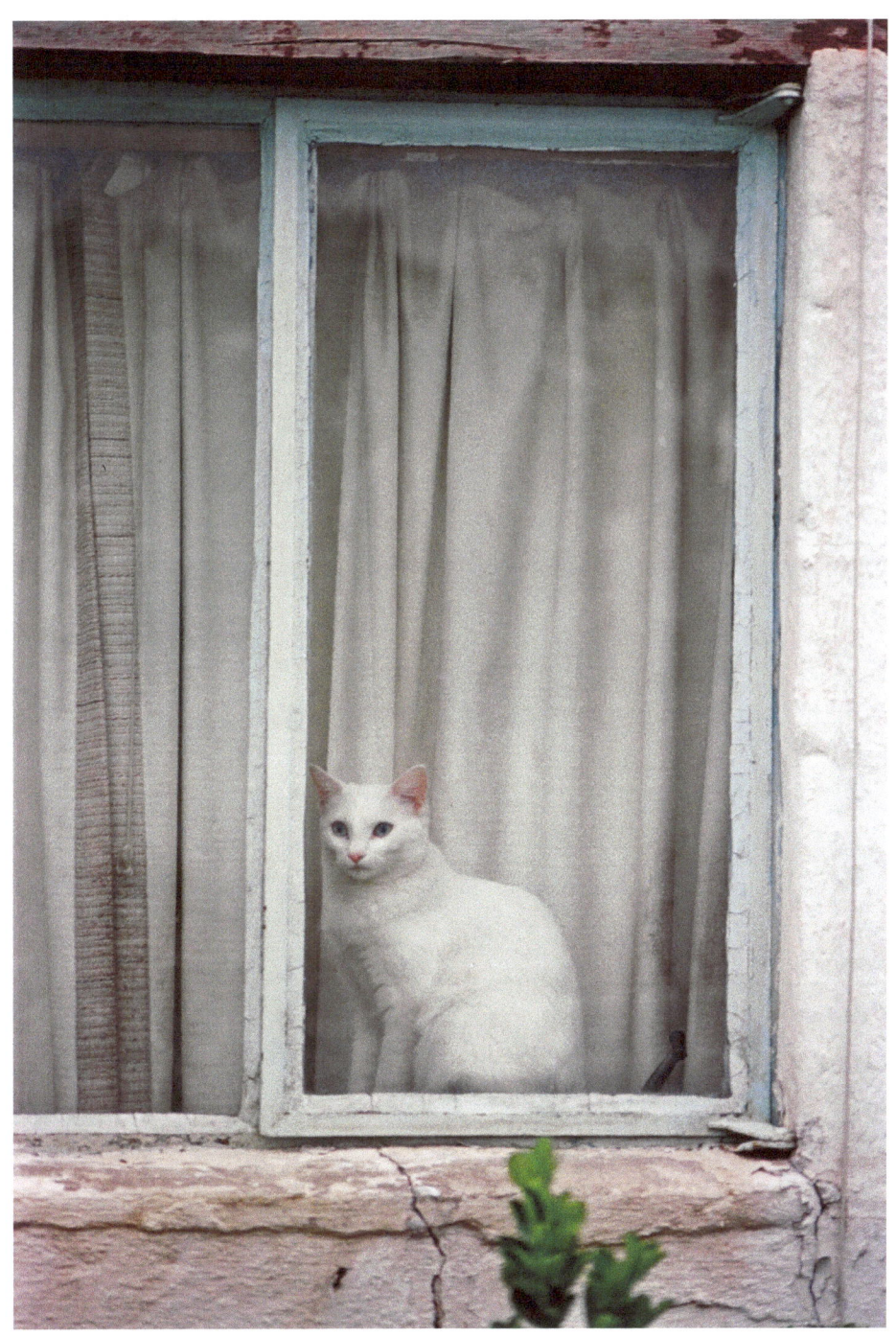

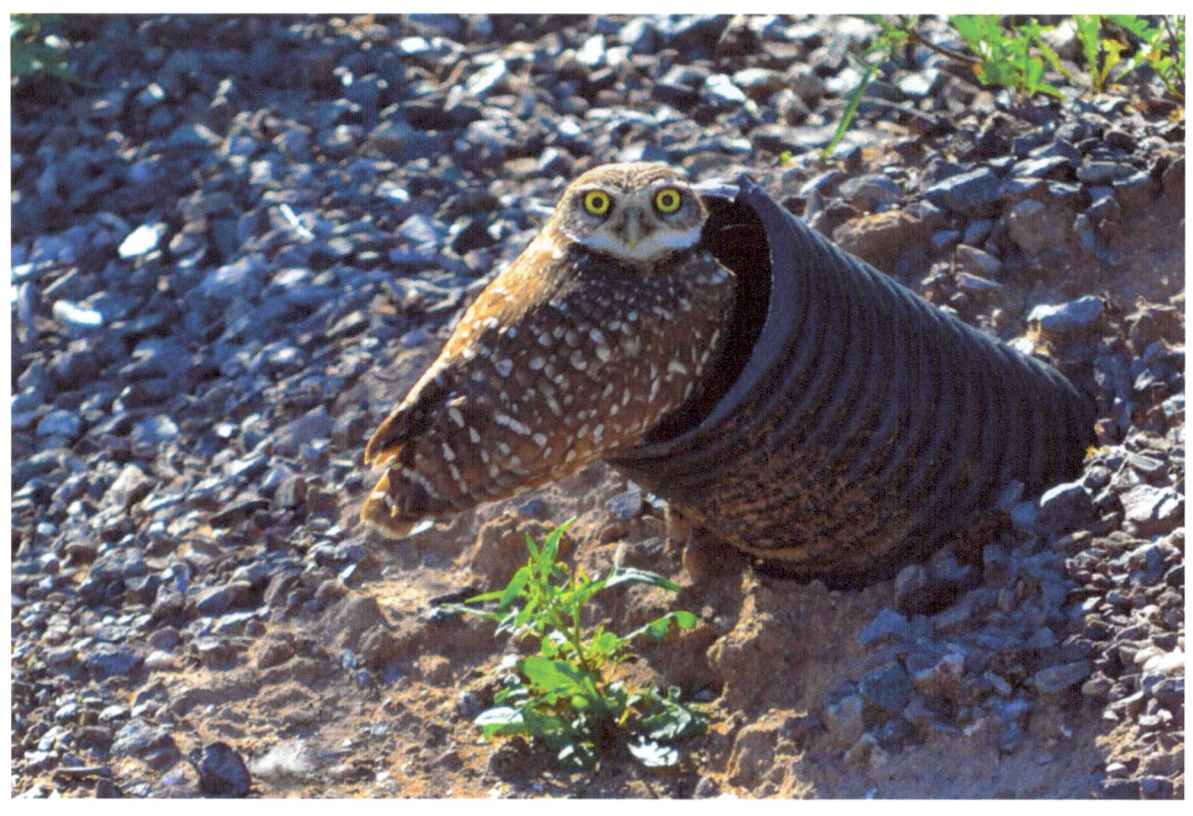

danger
tipping point
waiting

muscle
mania
slo-mo

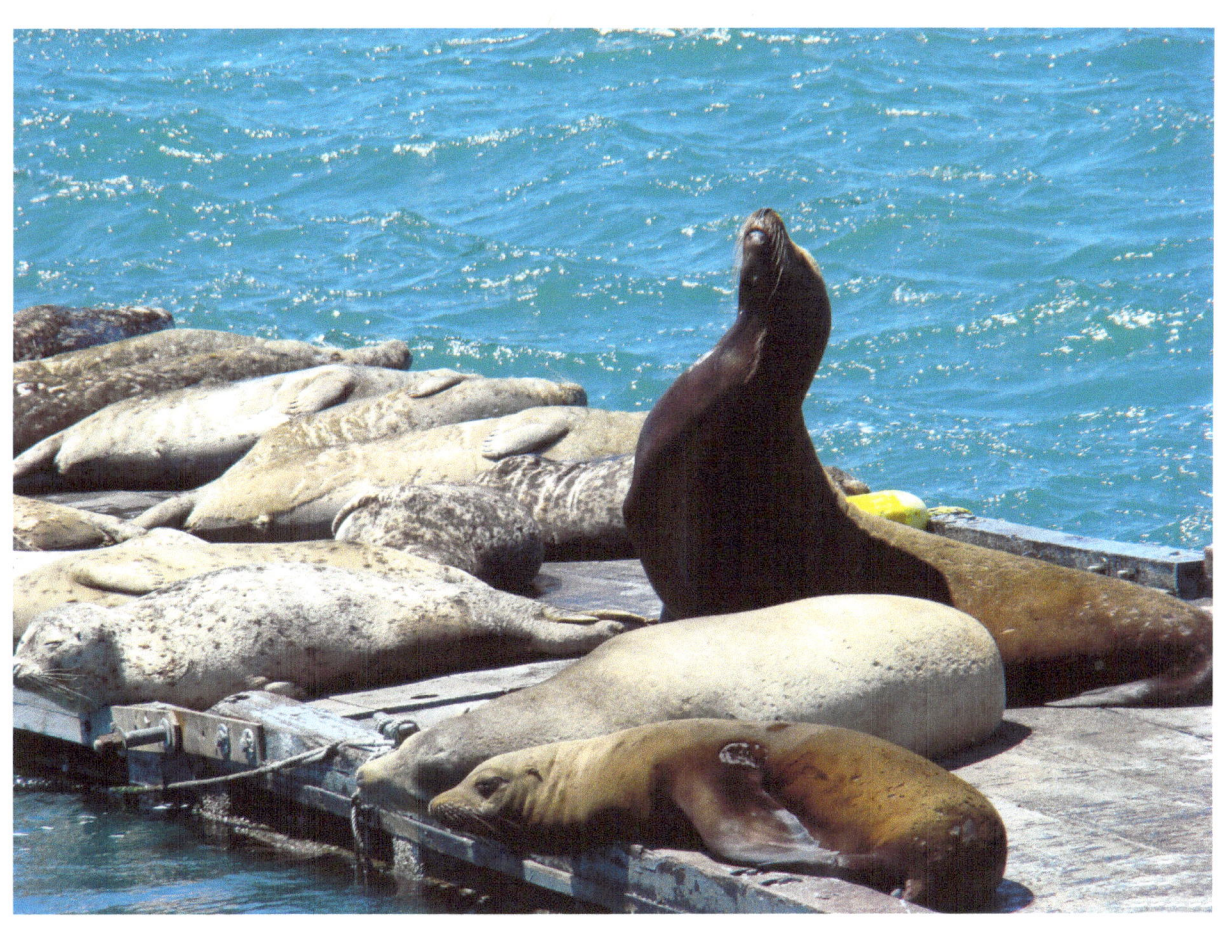

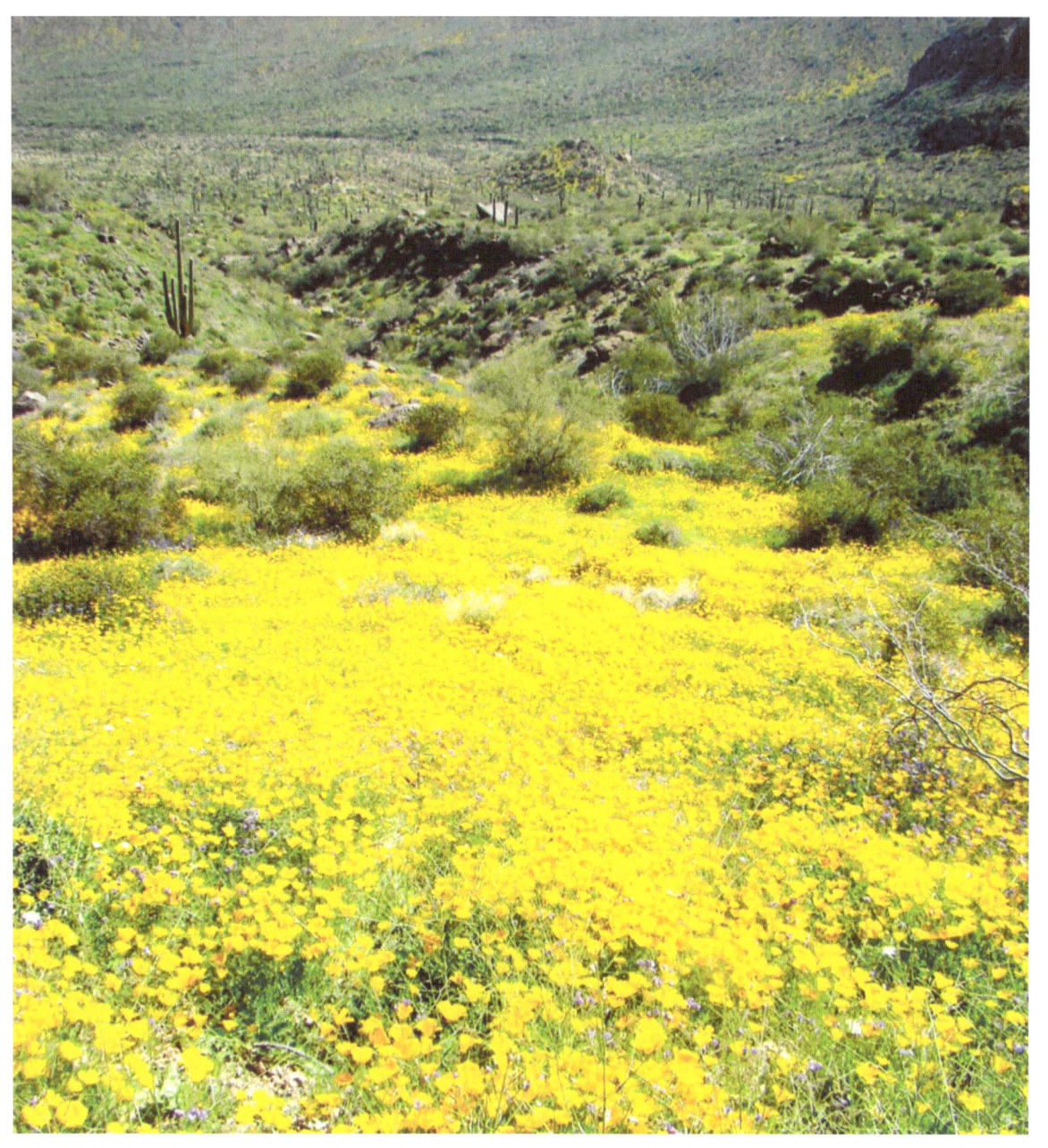

winter rains
desert
spring explosion

full moon
monsoon
mood

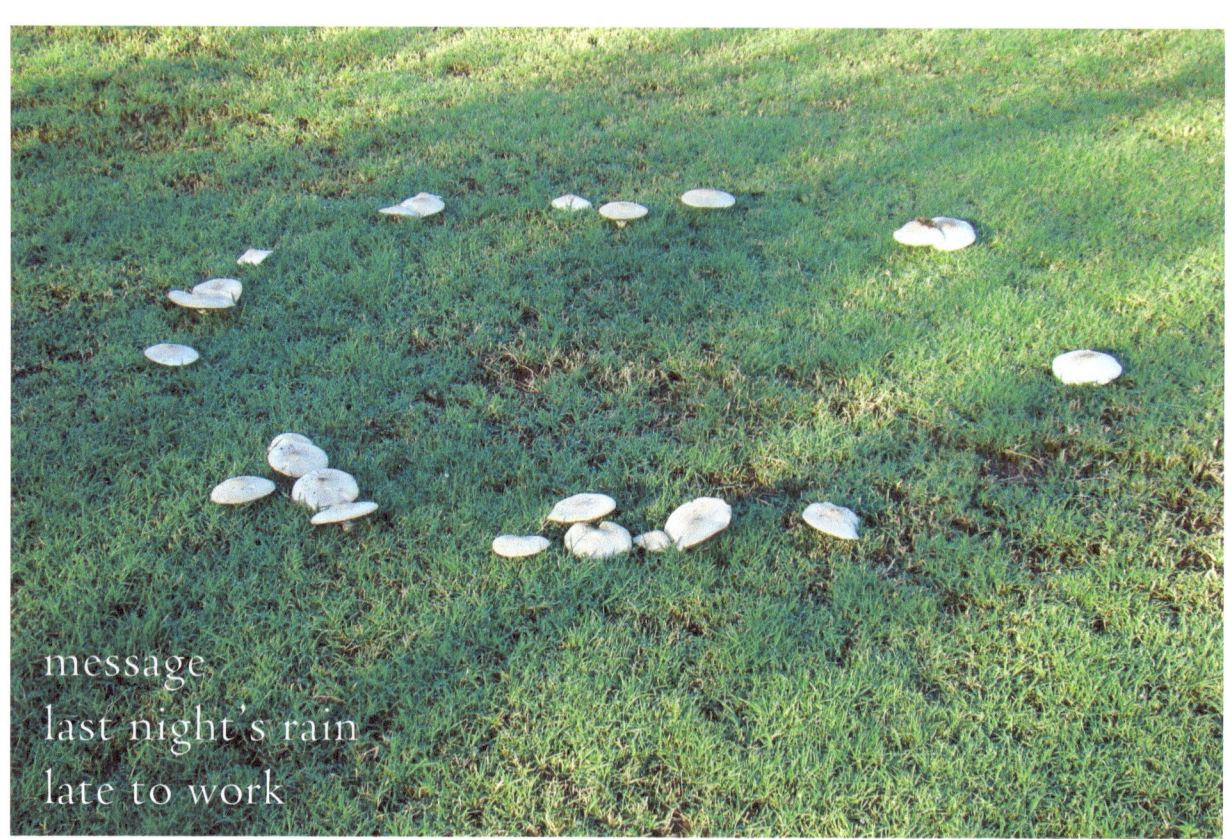

message,
last night's rain
late to work

breaching
spouting
playground

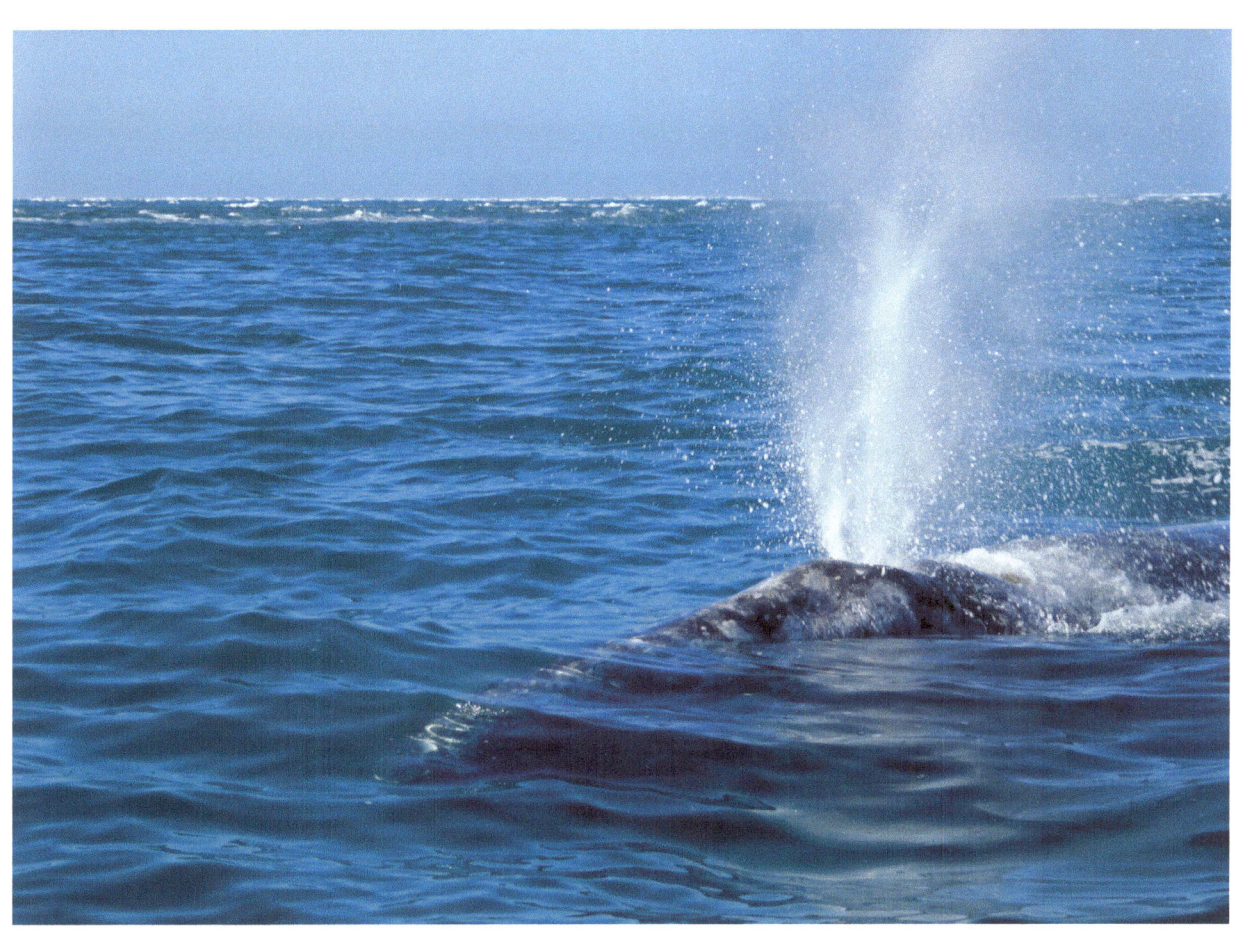

bottoms up
for
greens

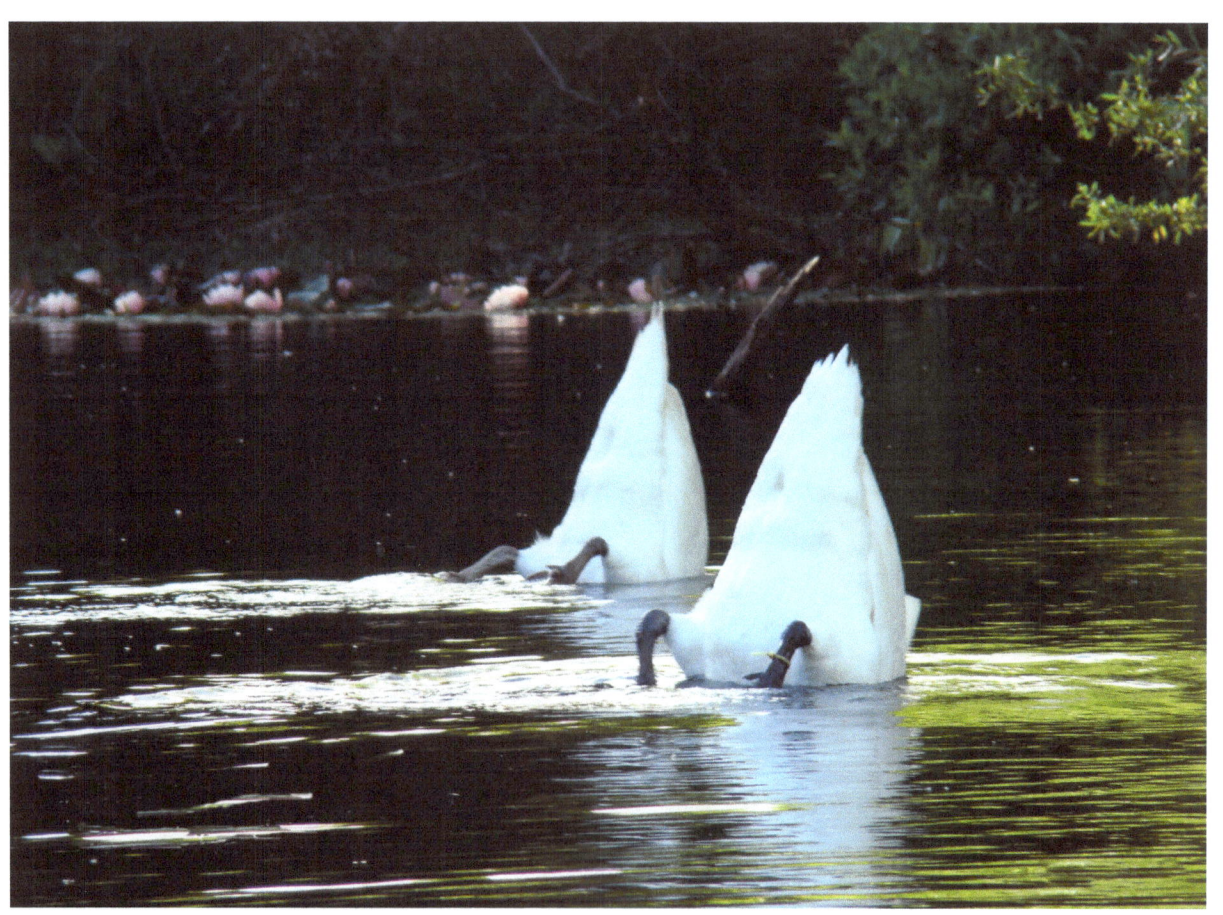

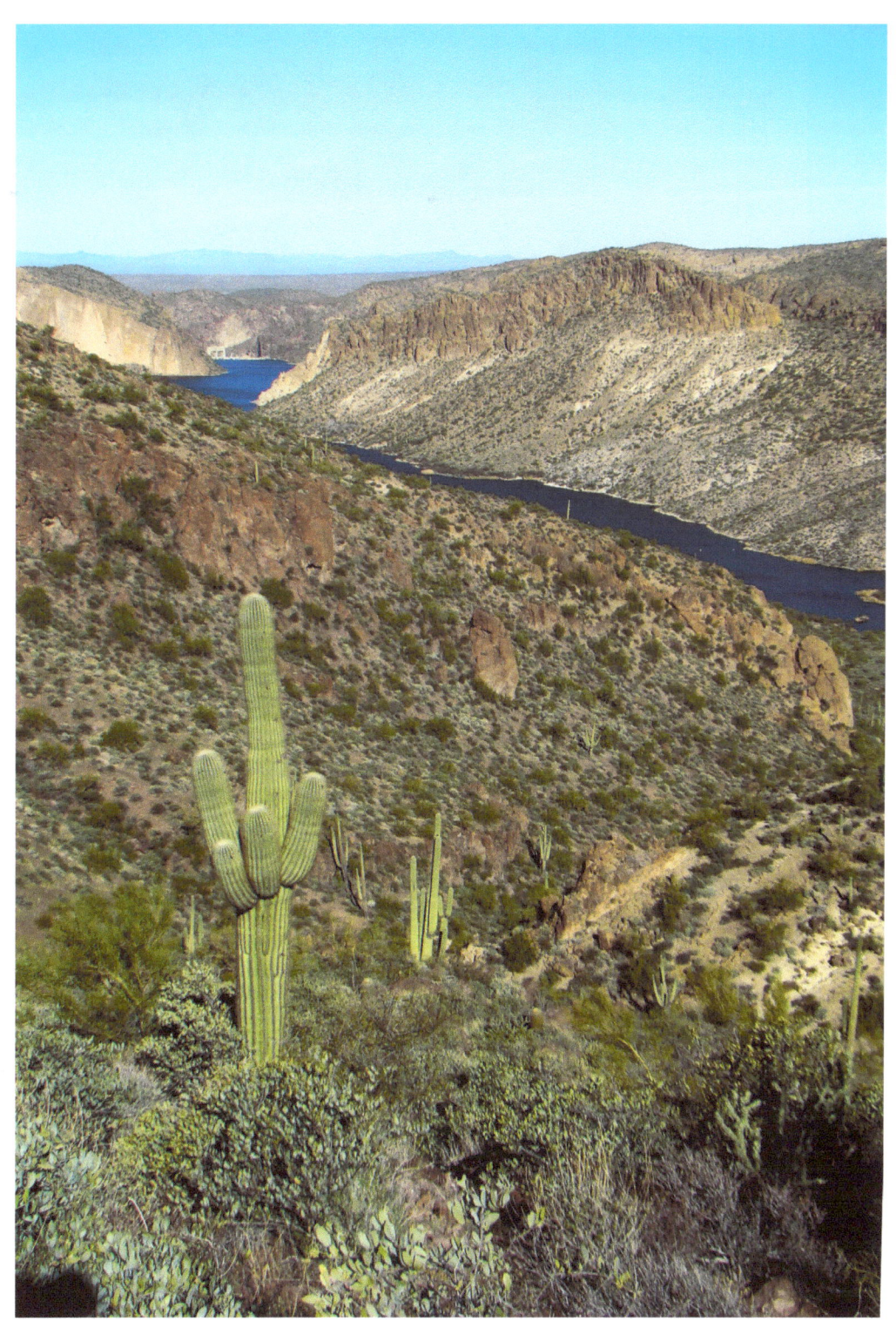

space
thirst
clean air

listen
muted
music

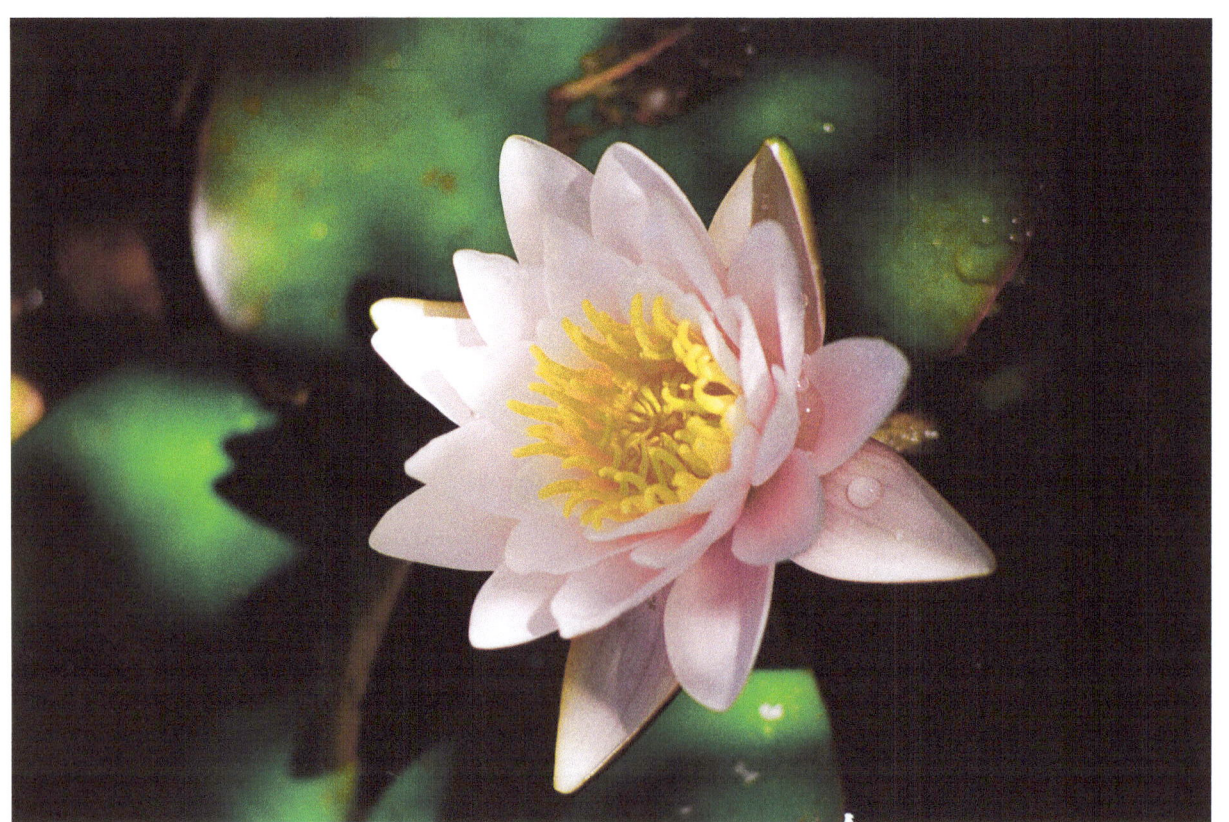

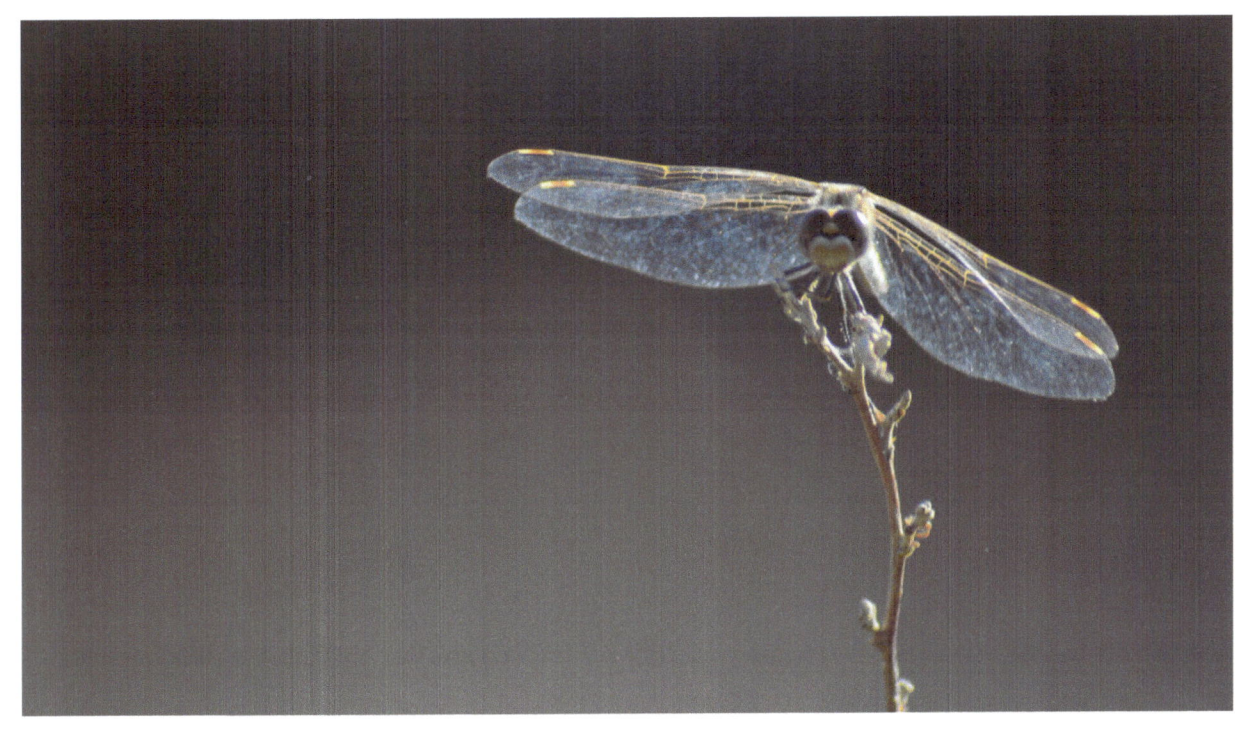

transparency
golden

beyond color
bang
door opens

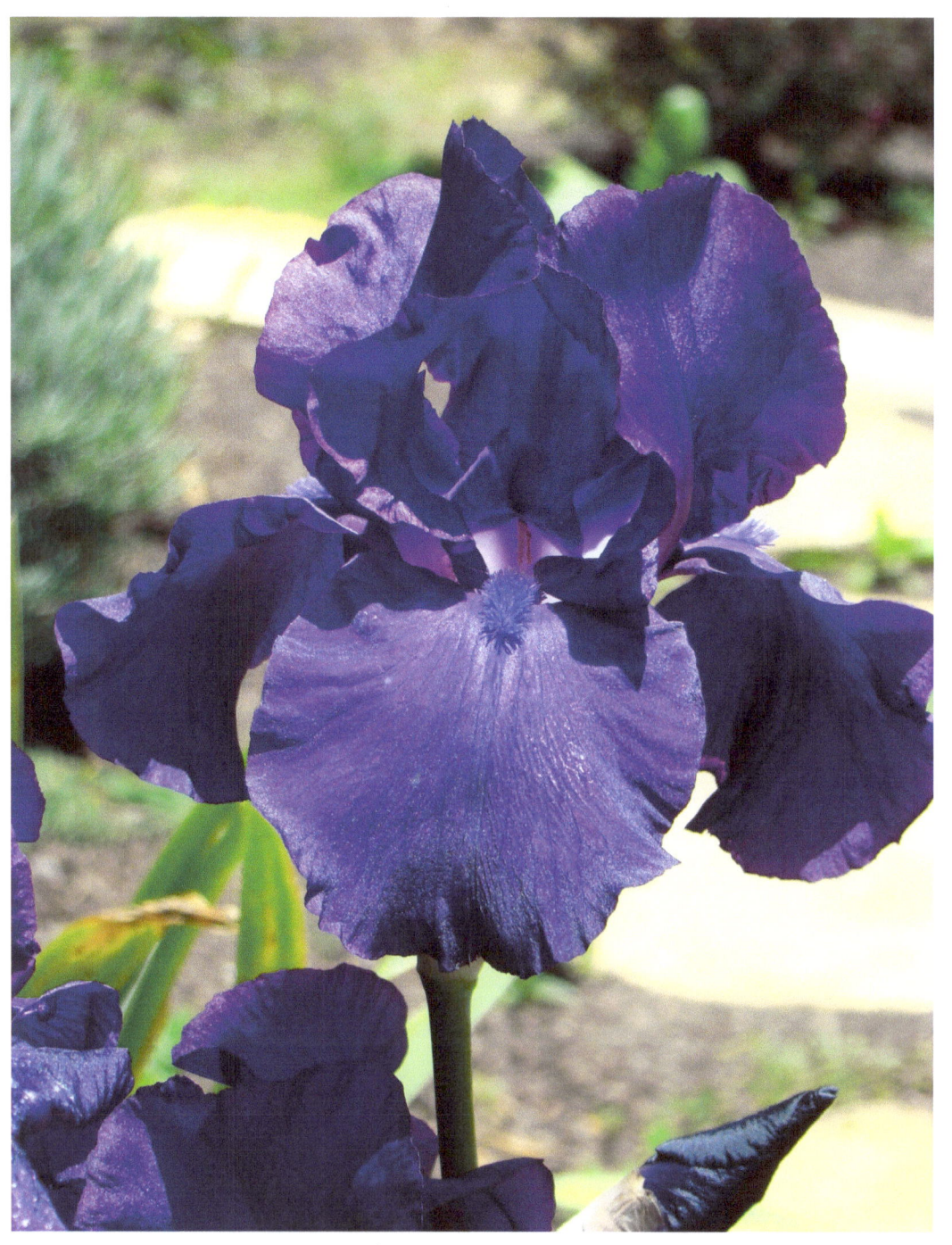

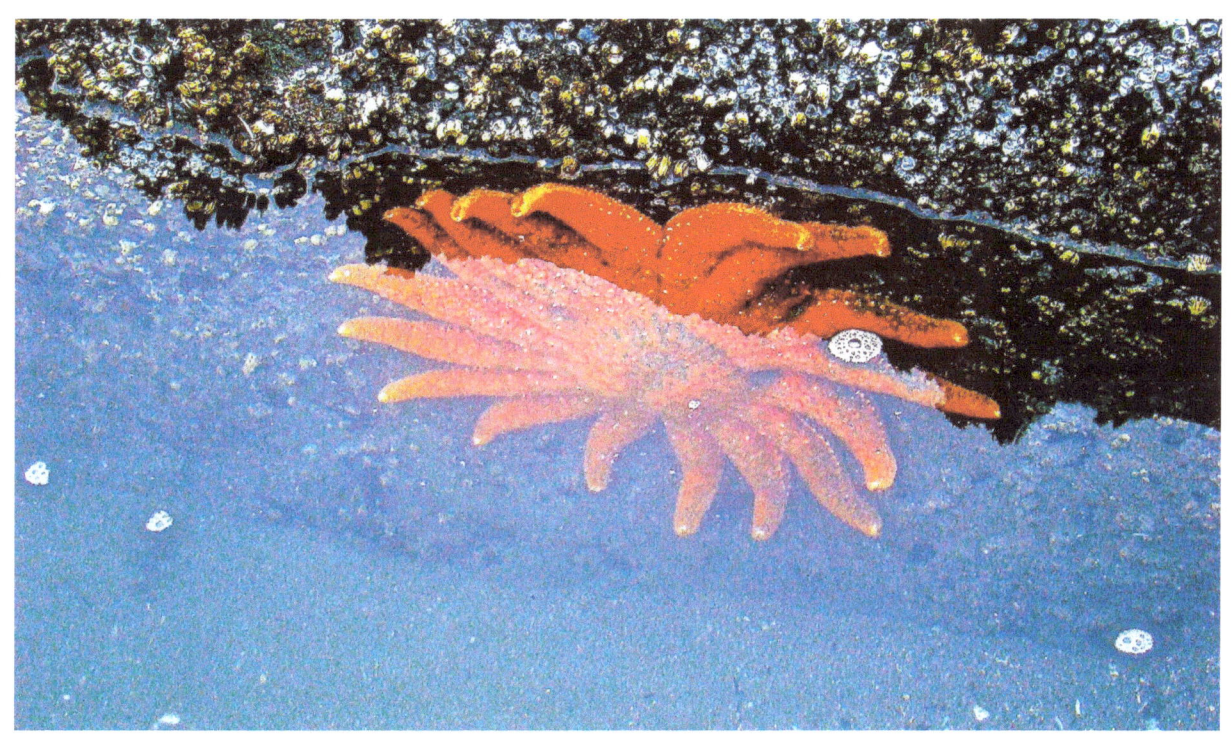

sunflower sea star
"Grandmother's Rock"
hugging

wrinkled
time
face

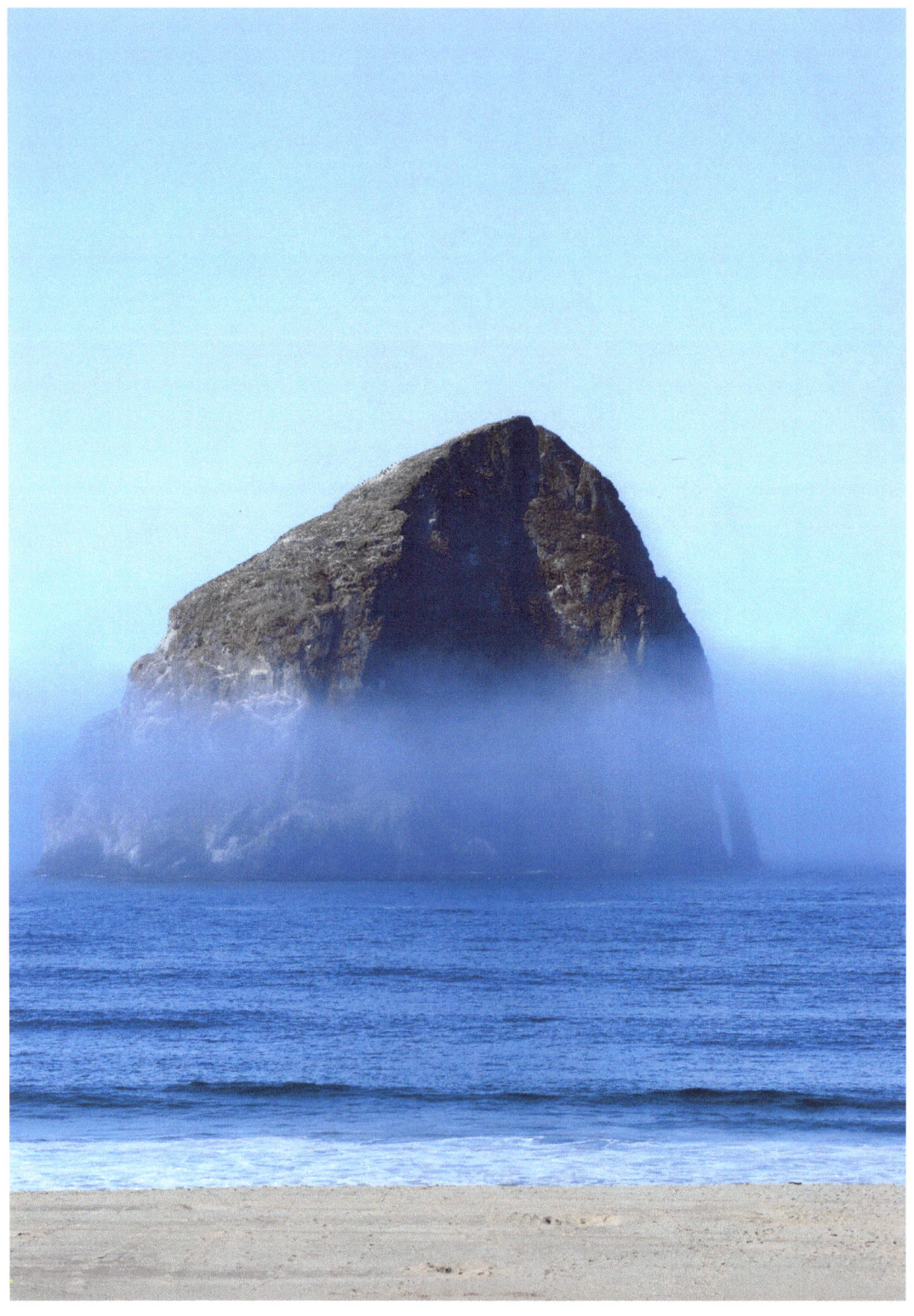

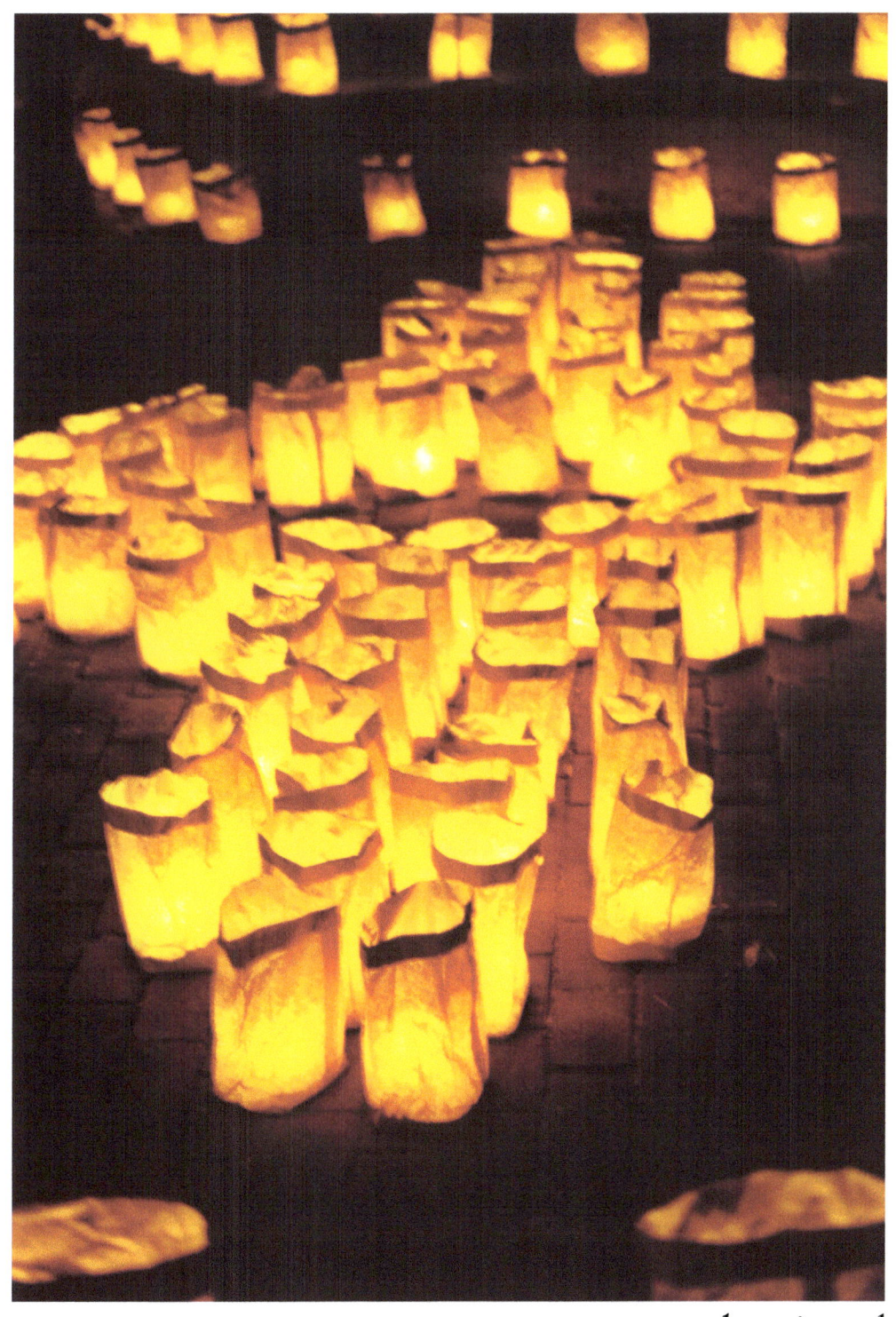

farolito
drawing the power
sharing the light

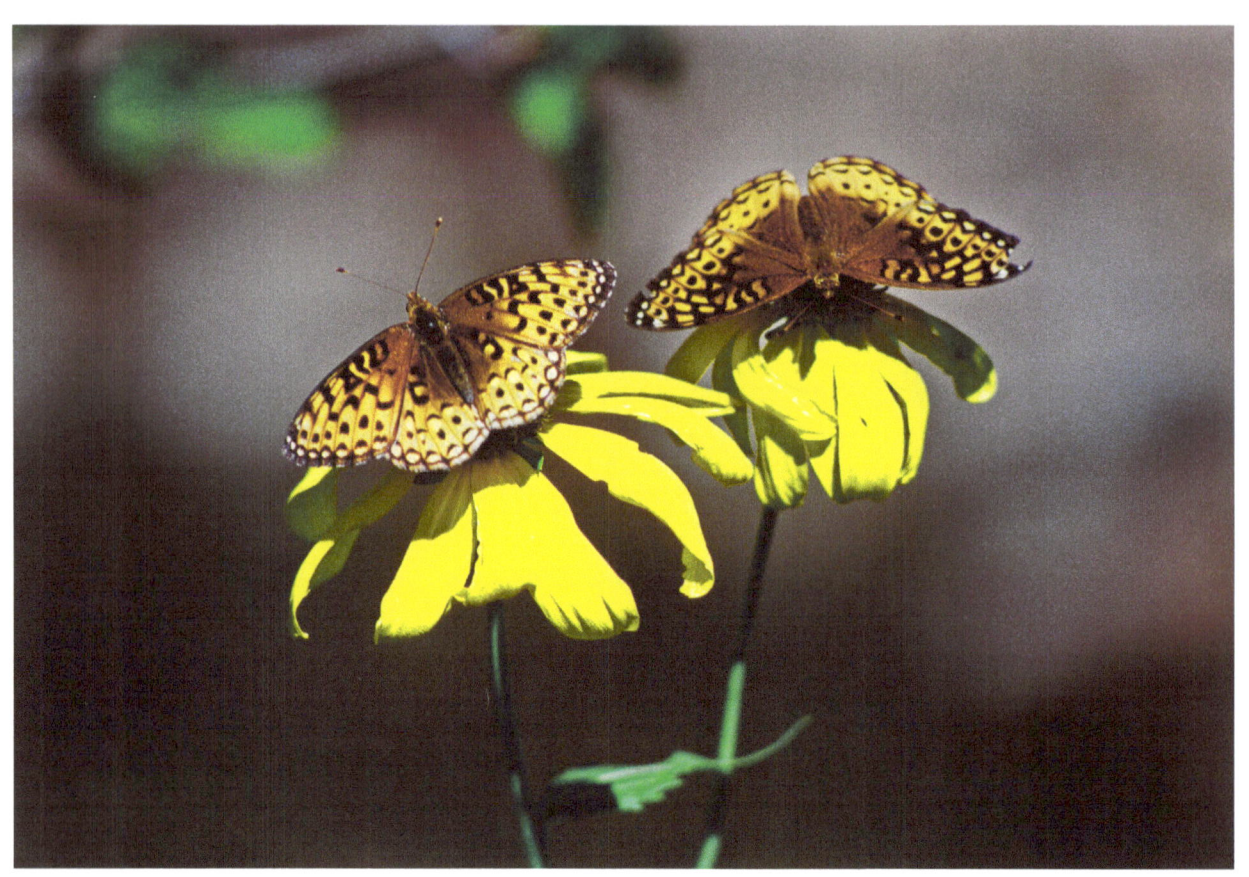

grande
nectar
flight

passage
hundreds of years
legacy

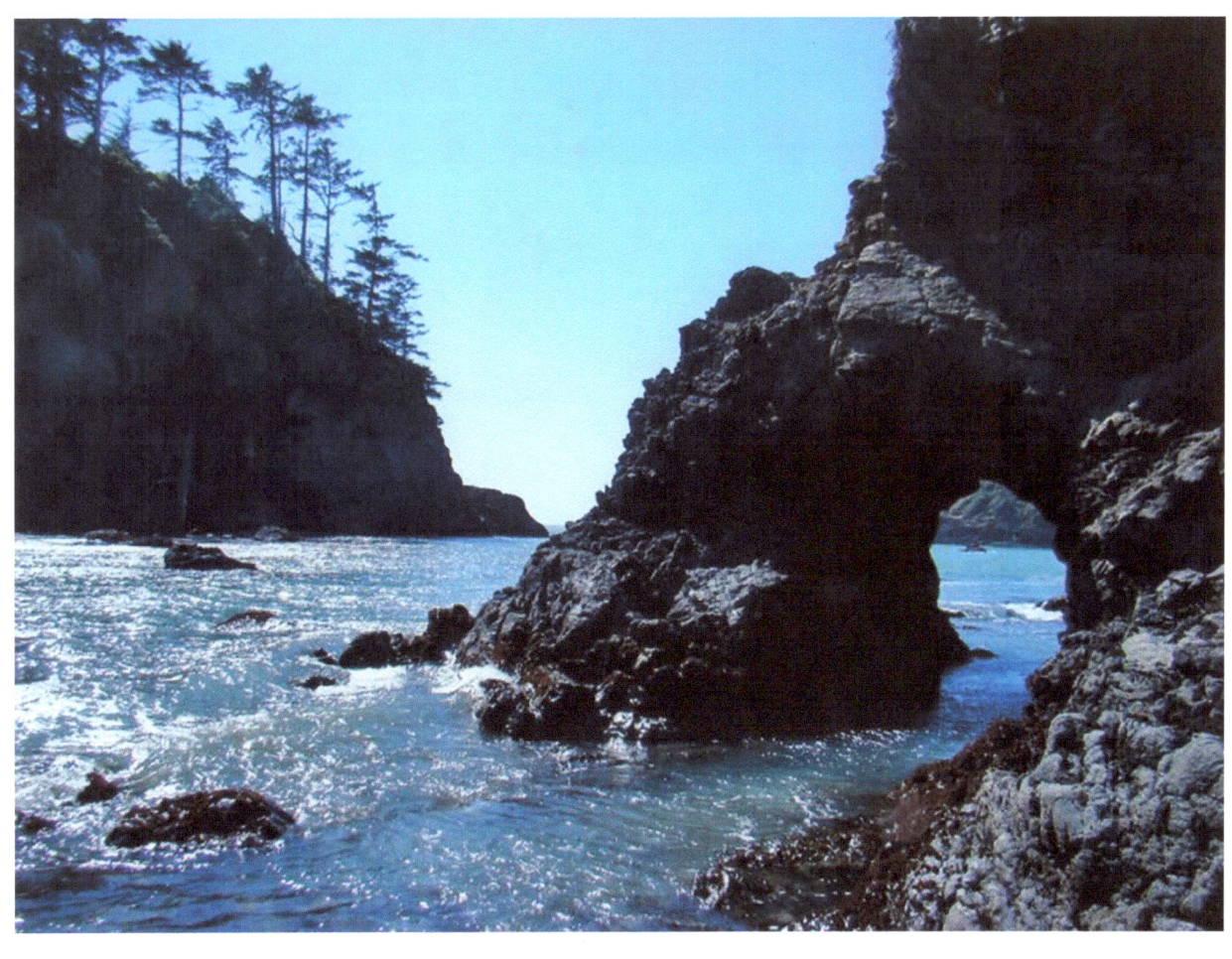

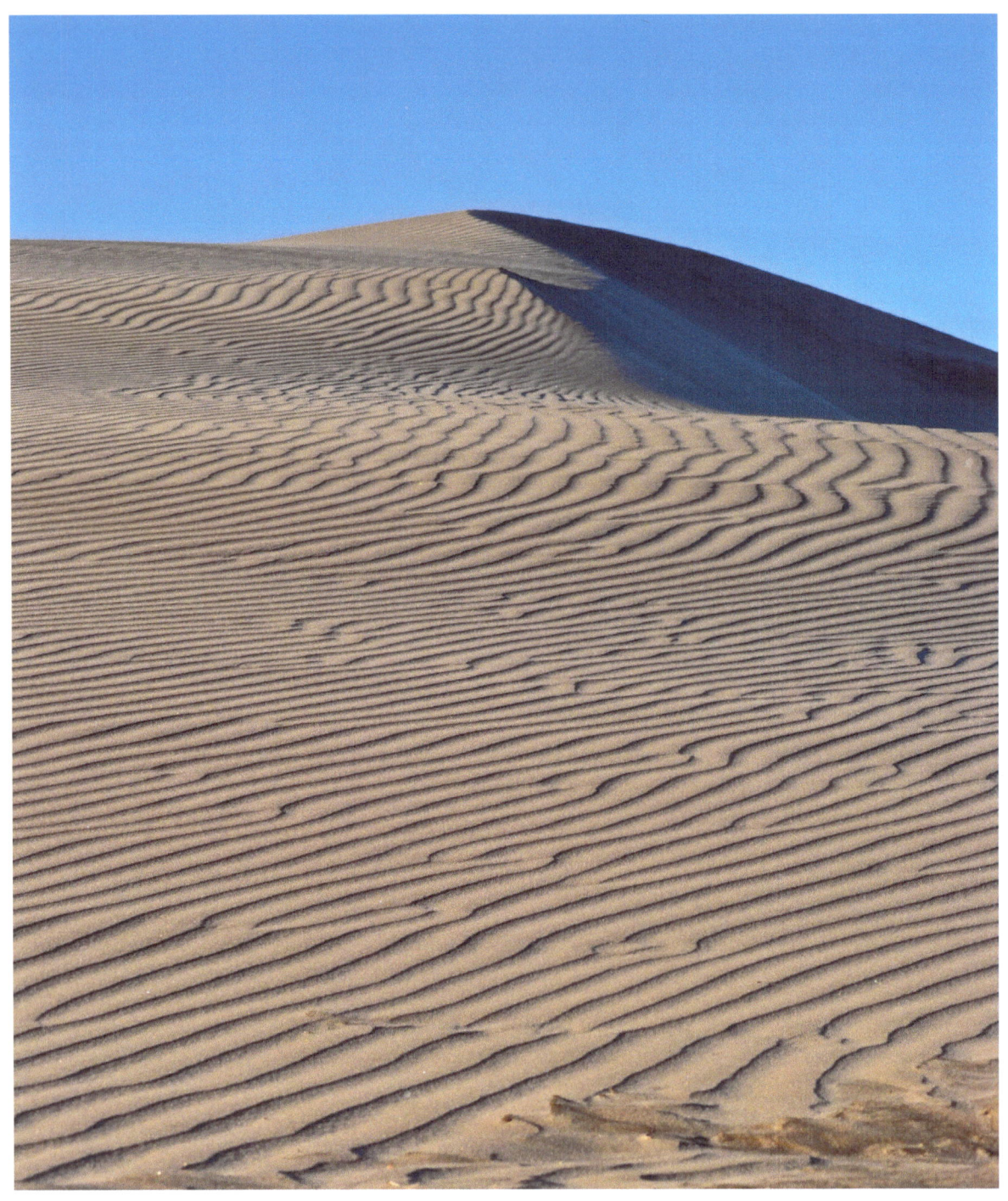

grooving
harmony
brain waves

after its breach
gray whale's
footprint

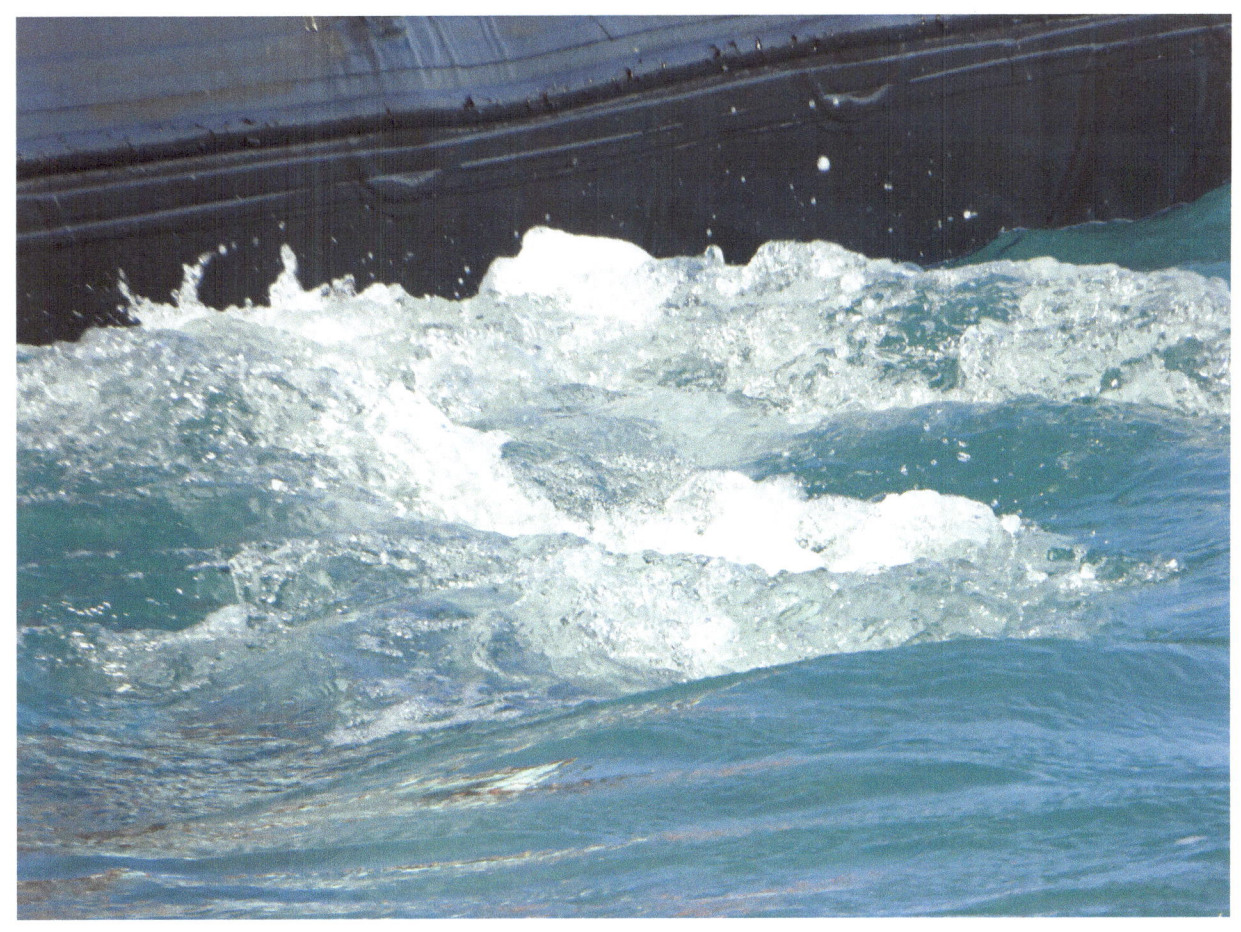

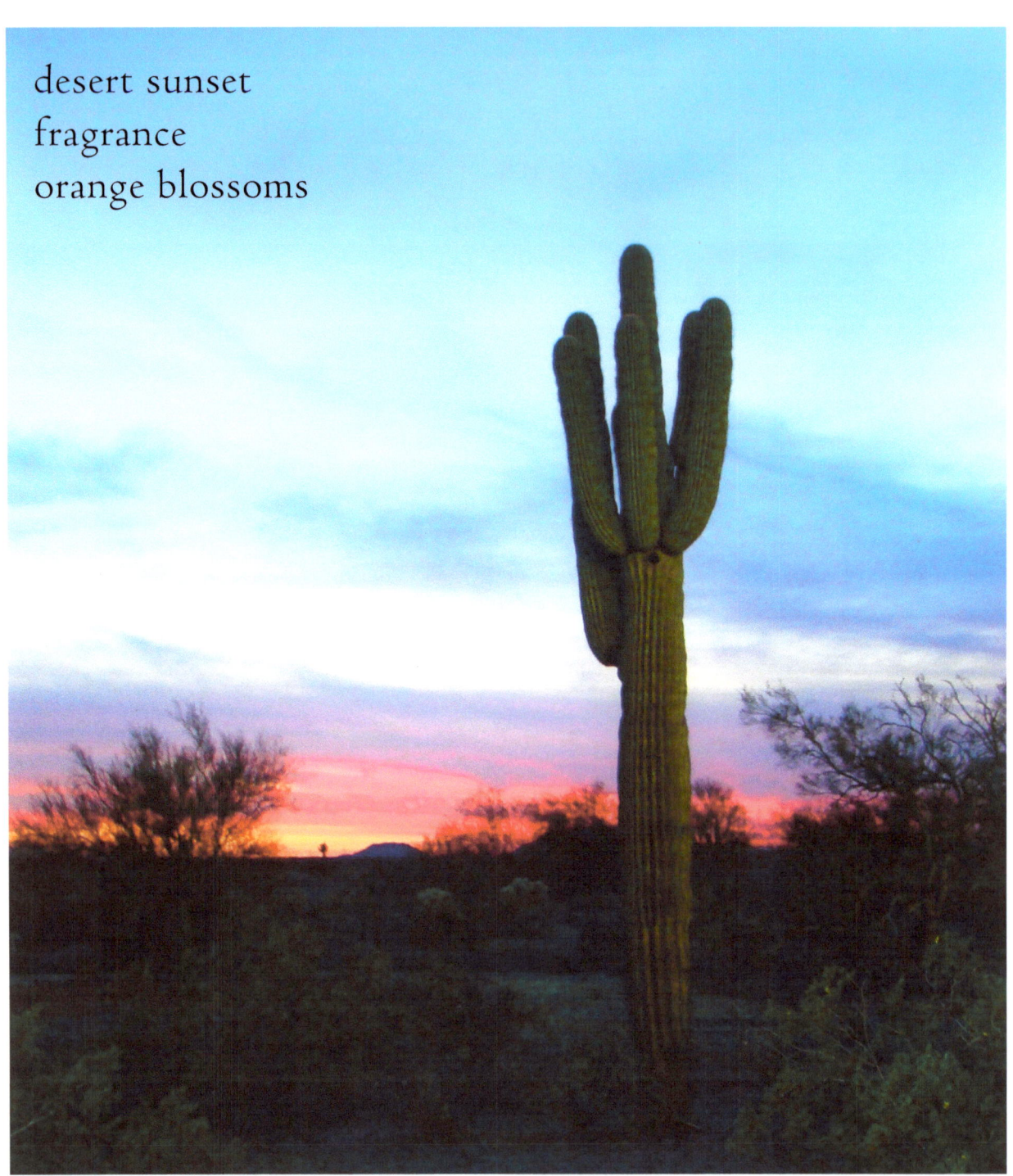

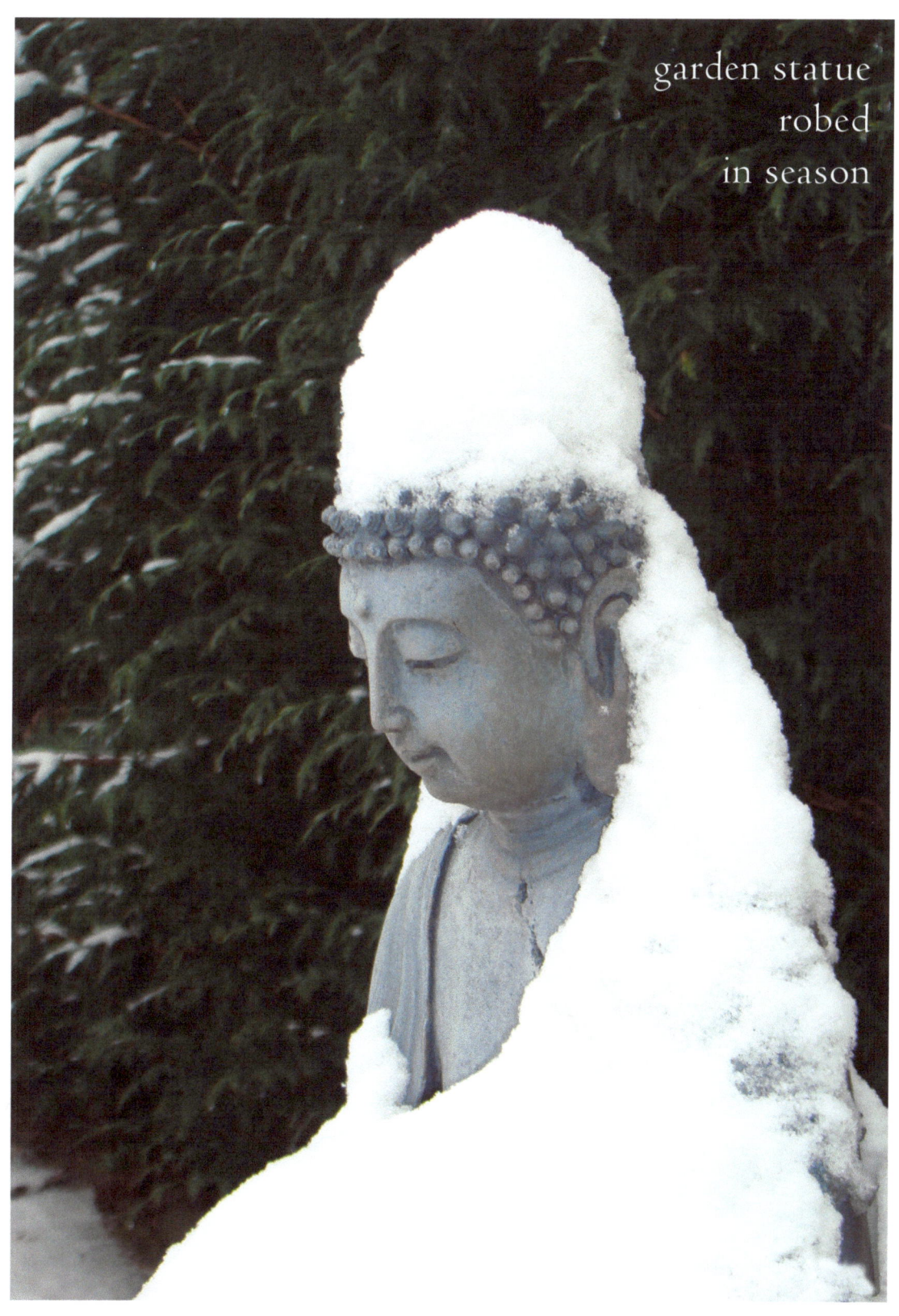

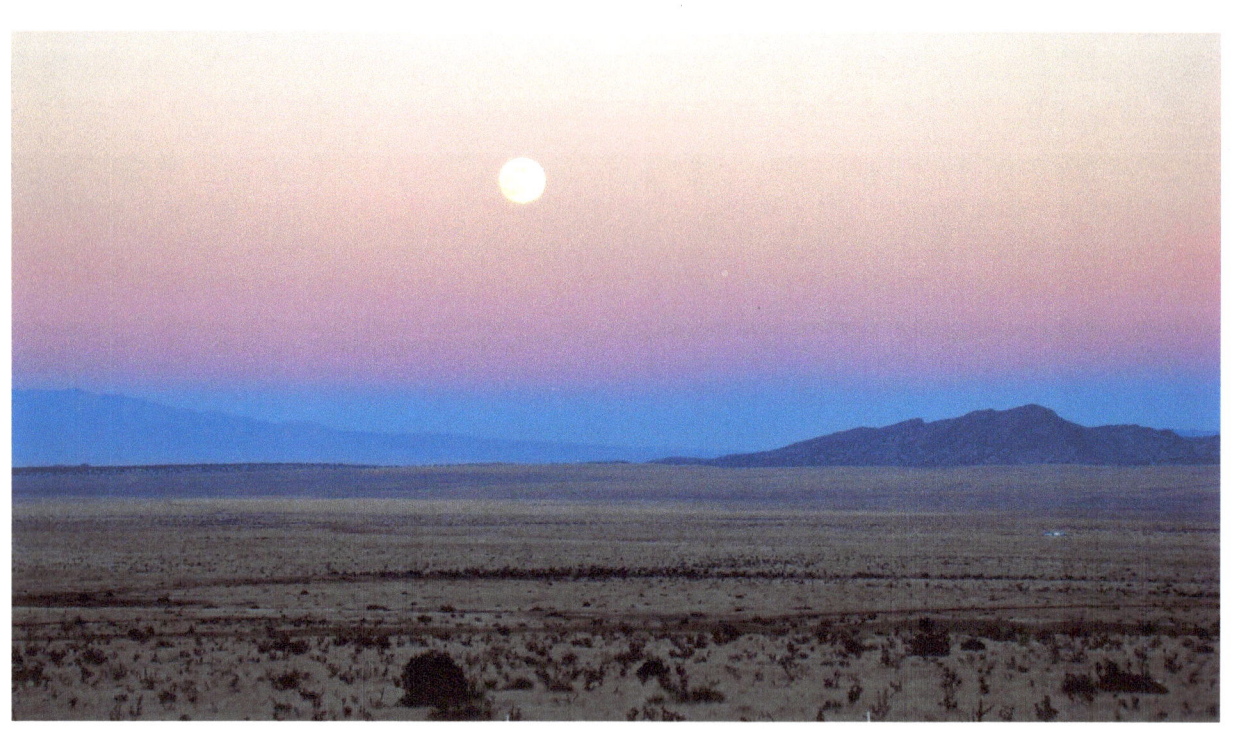

rising
fire circle of friends
gong

ice cream cones
arthritis
childhood friends

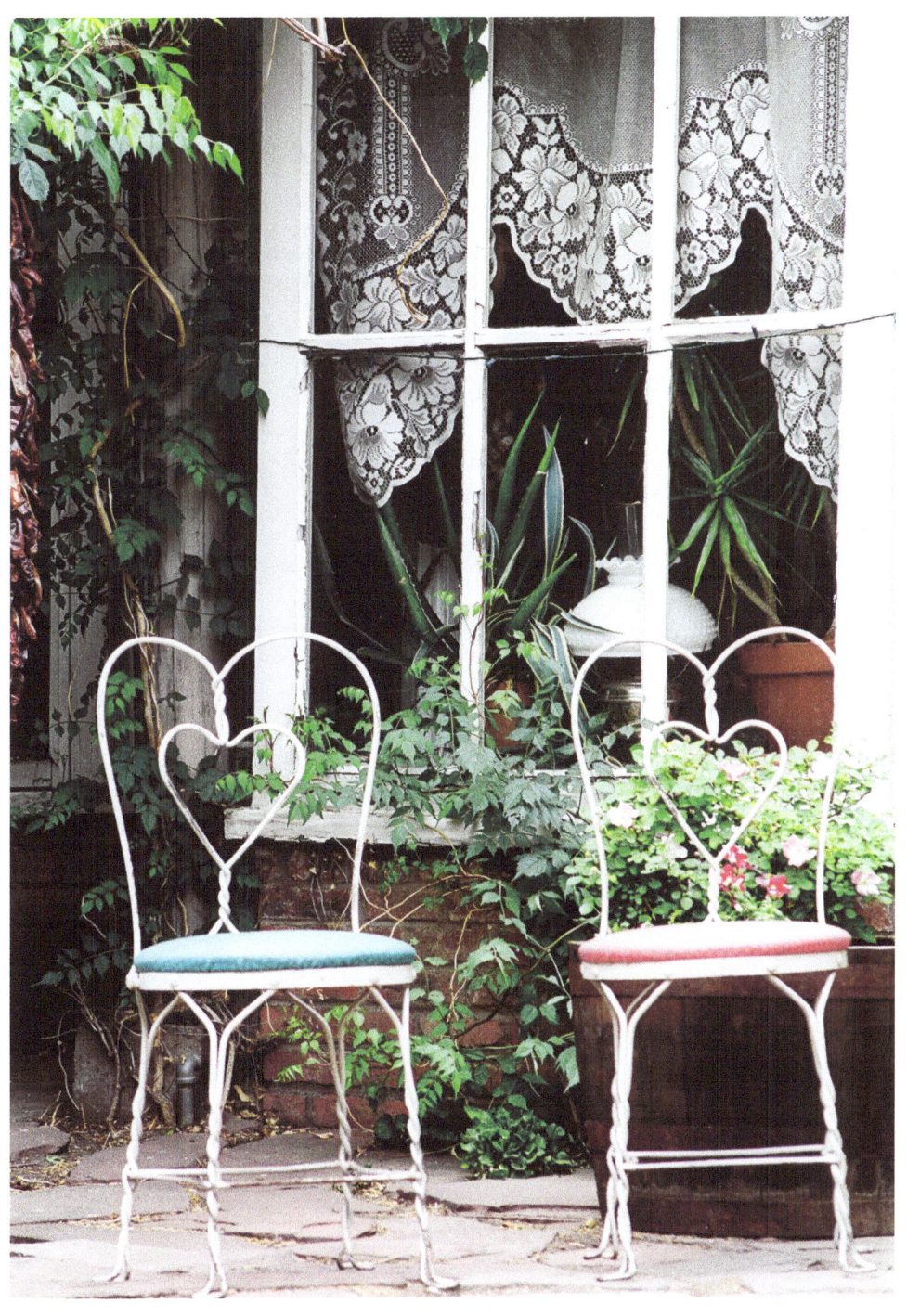

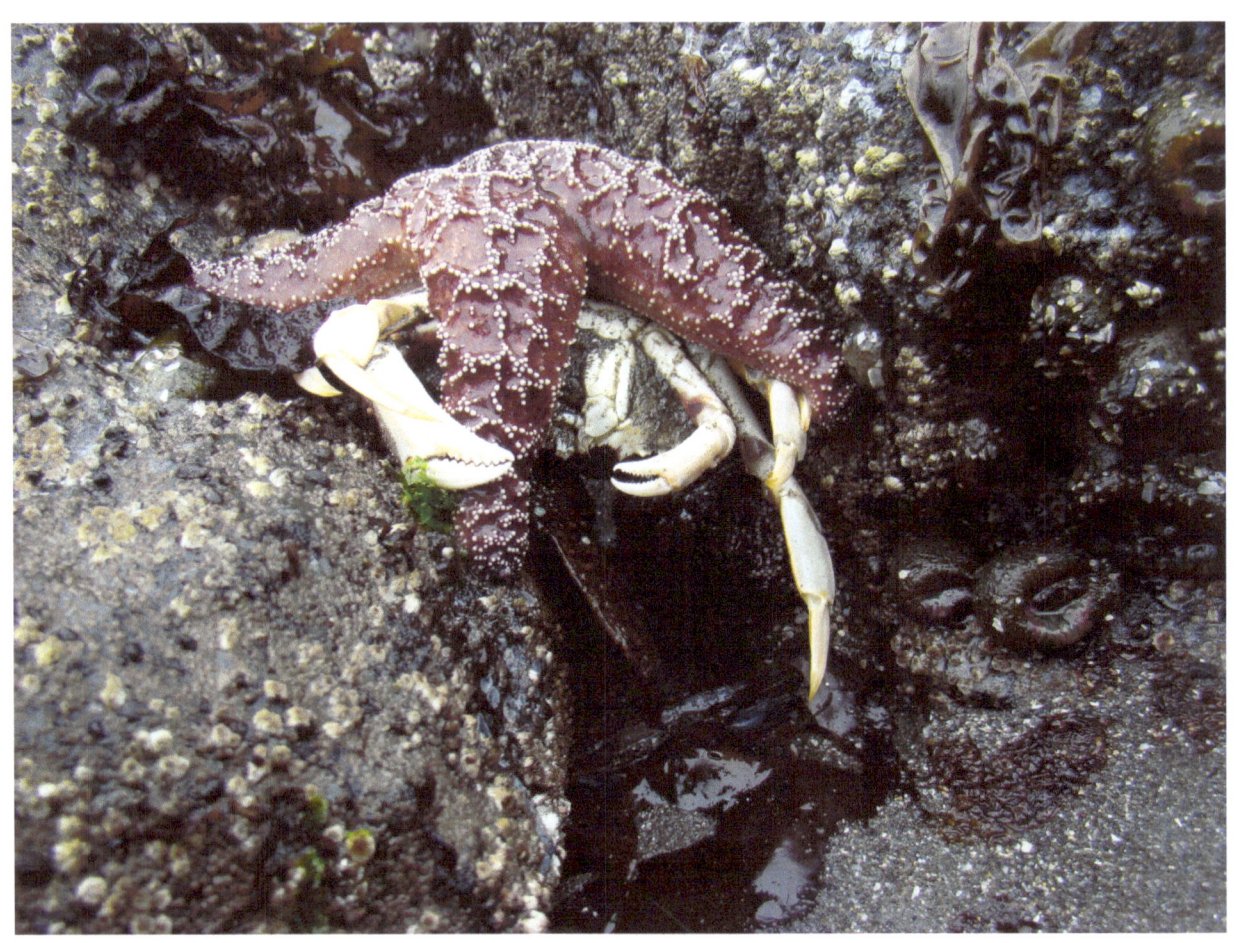

picnic
at
low tide

holding on
in the float
full and shallow

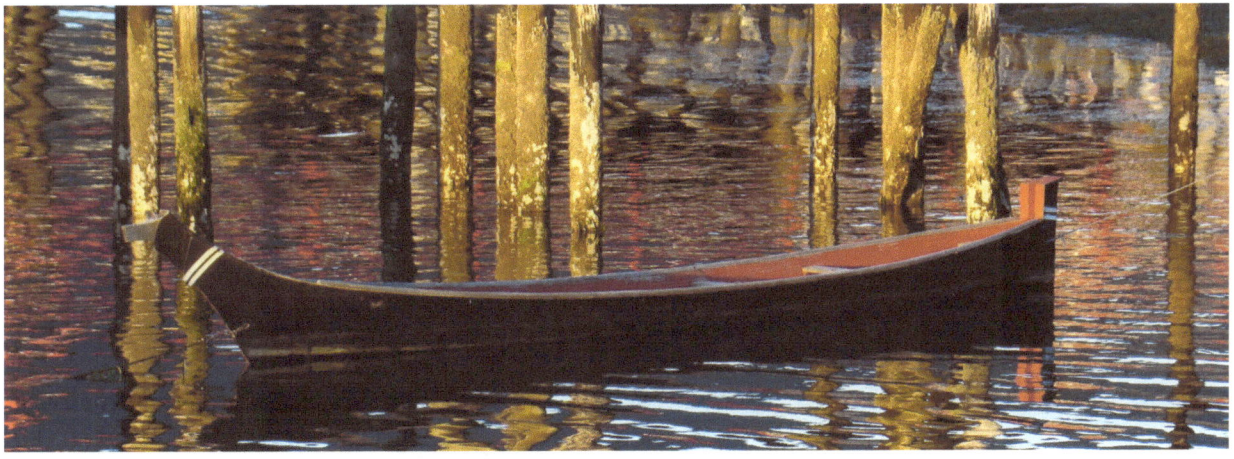

partial pier
hurricane
new use

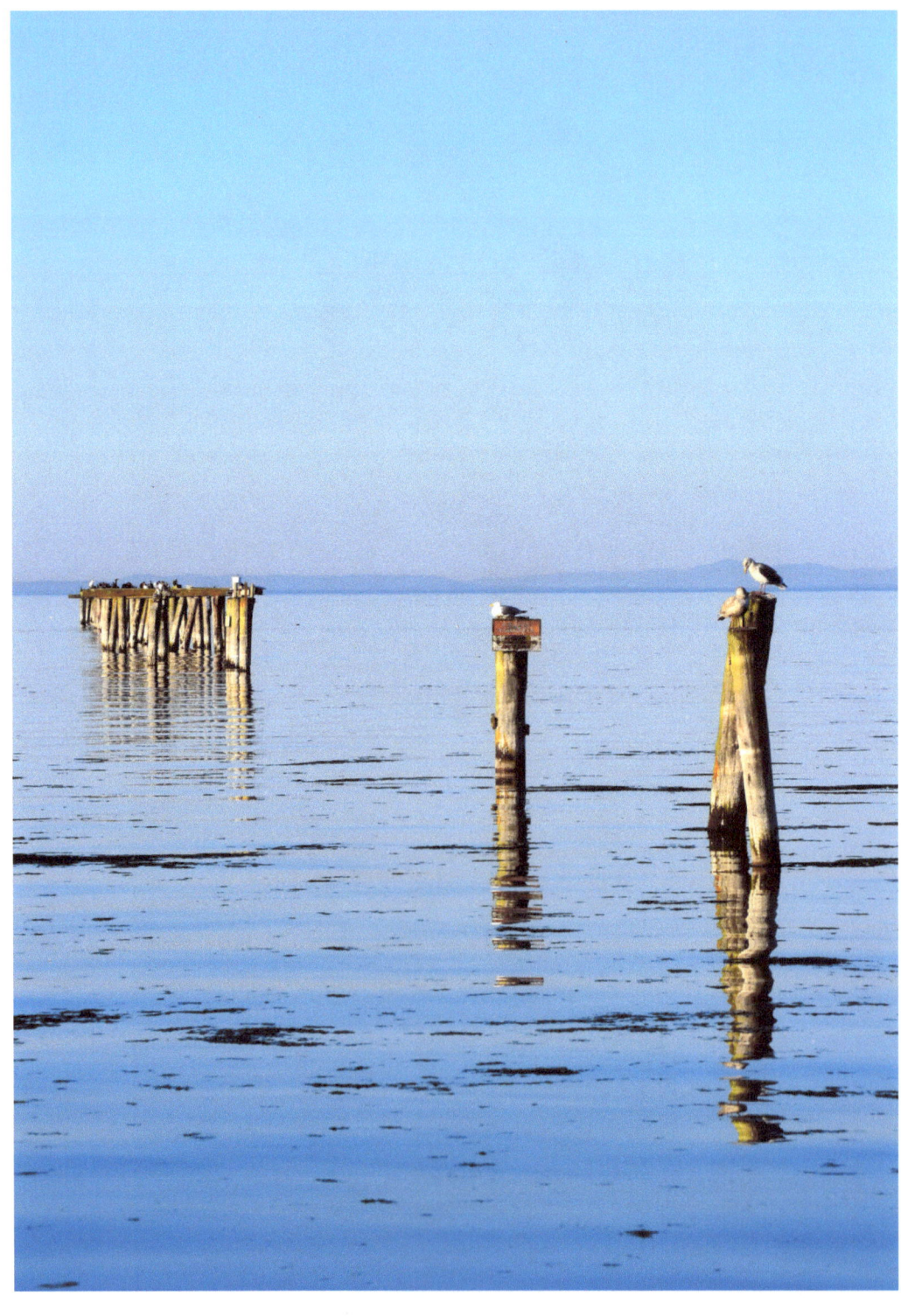

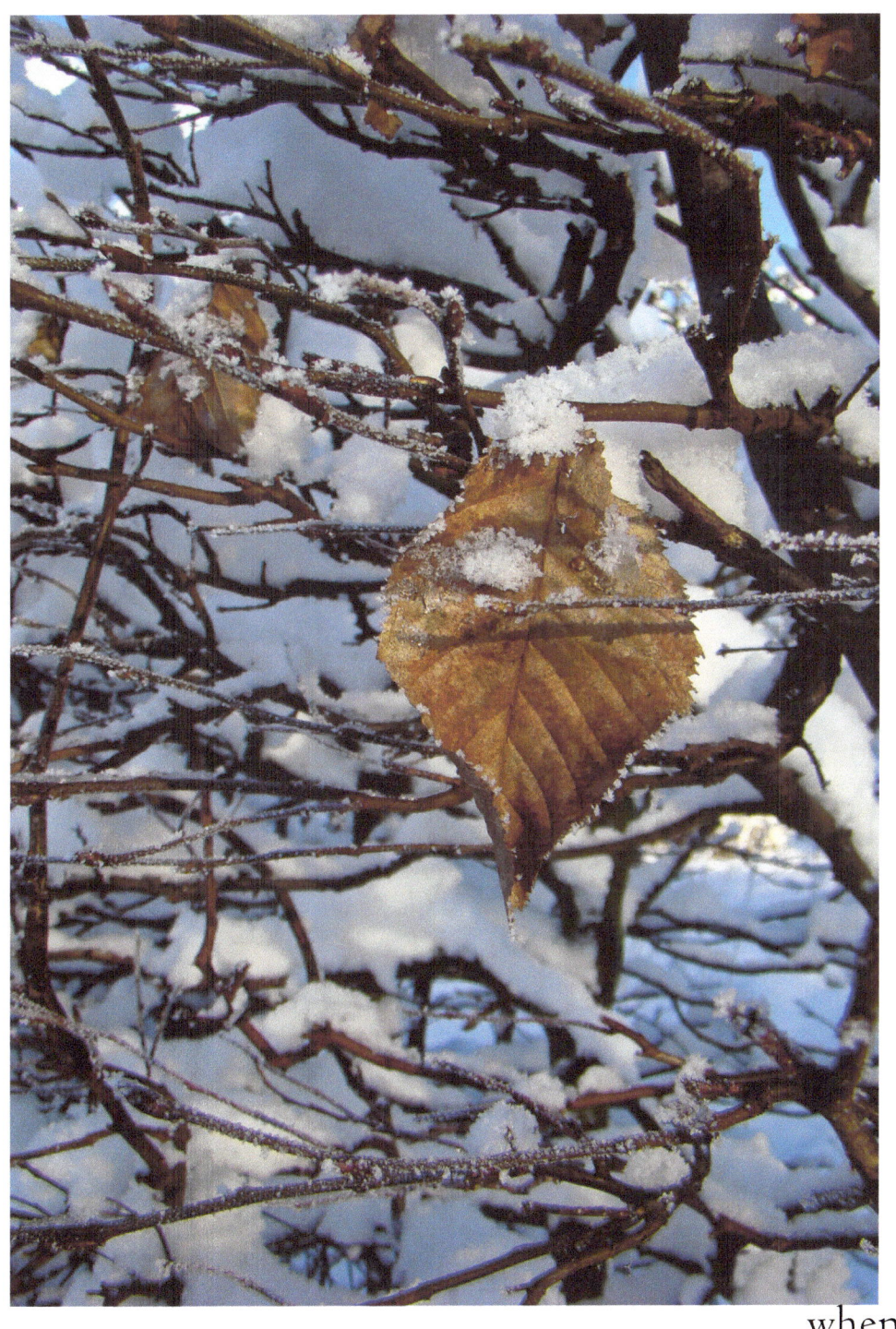

when change
comes calling
hanging on

searching
bifocal
clarity

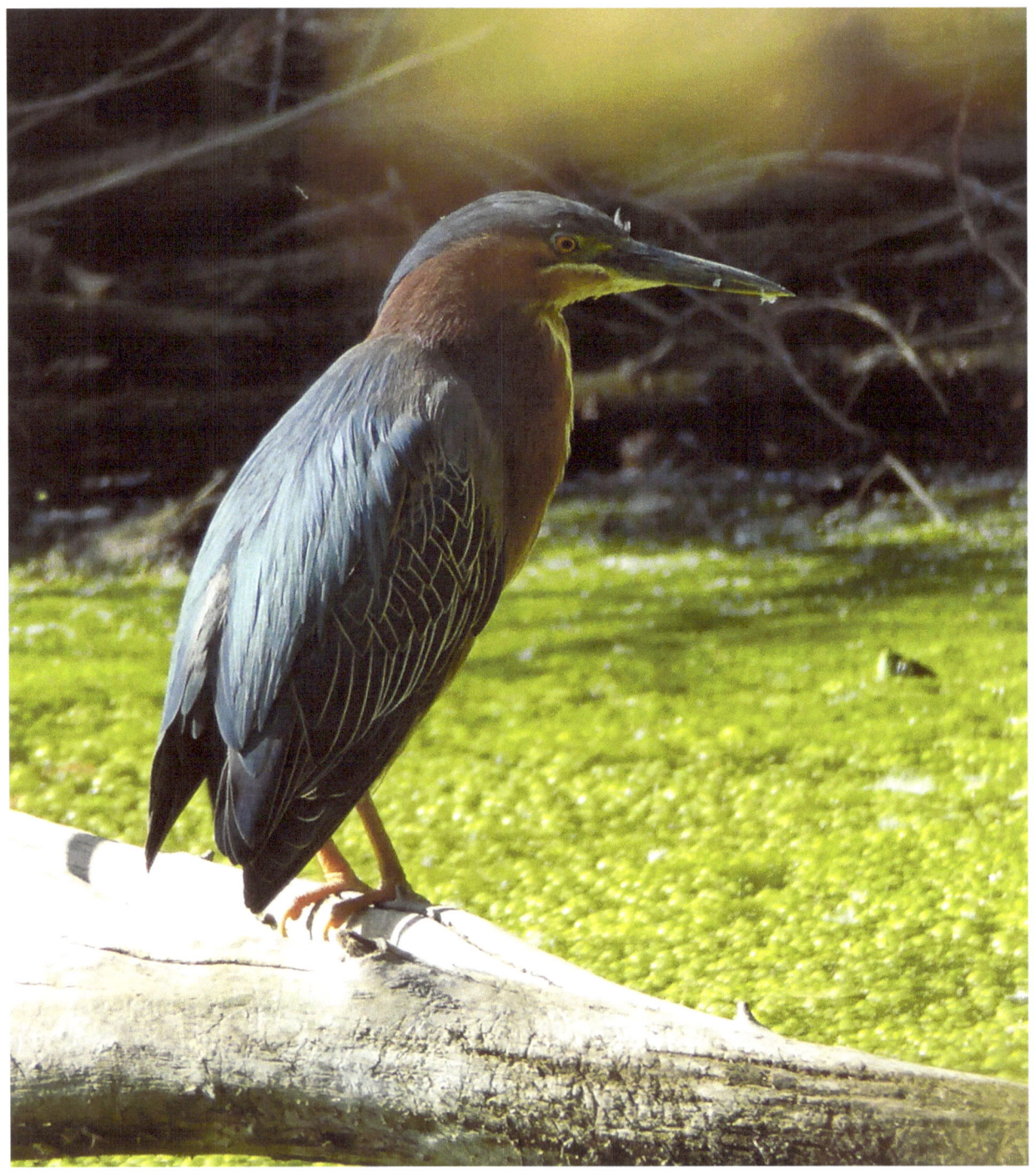

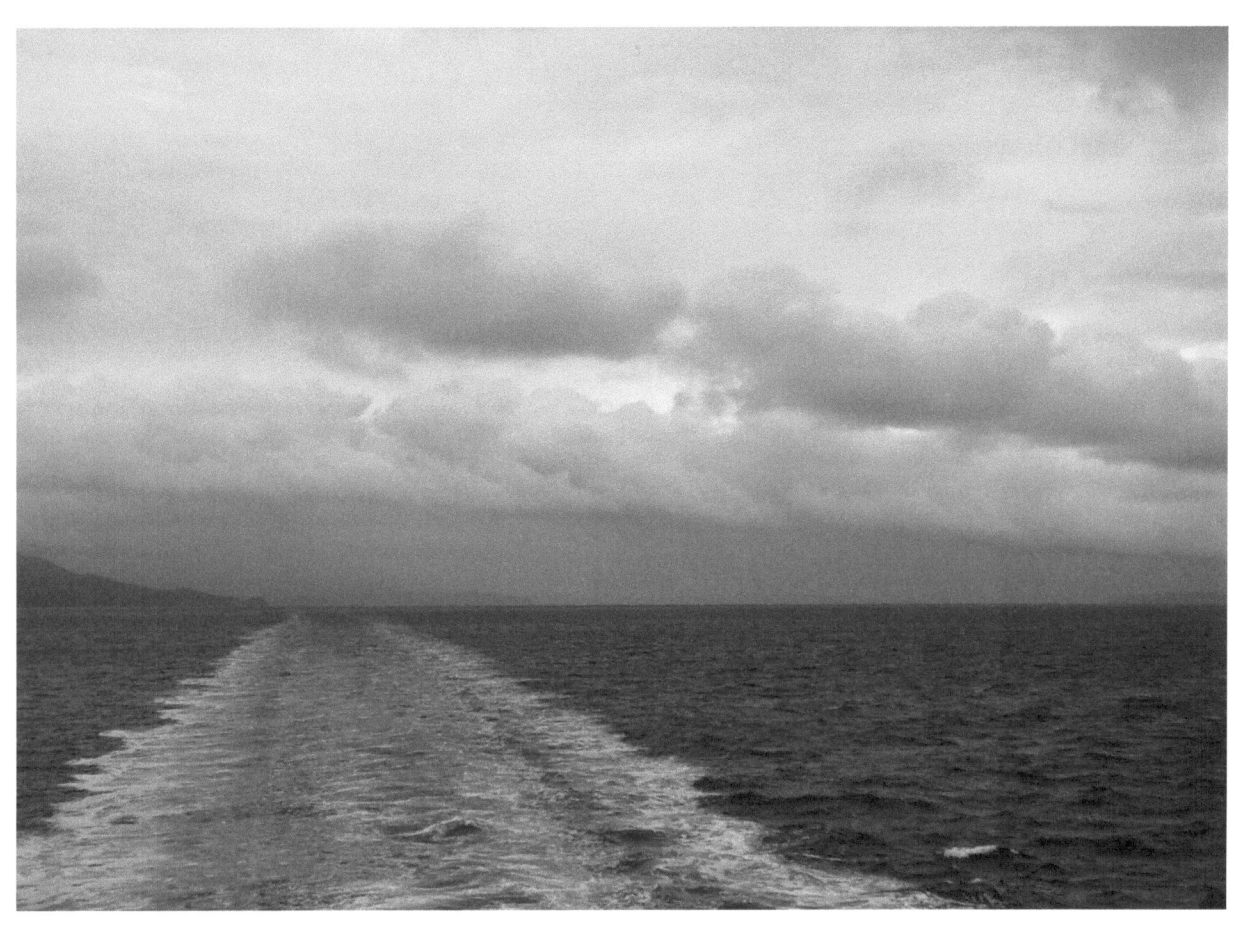

weathering
axe
cape super

moon song
canyon wren
ears smile

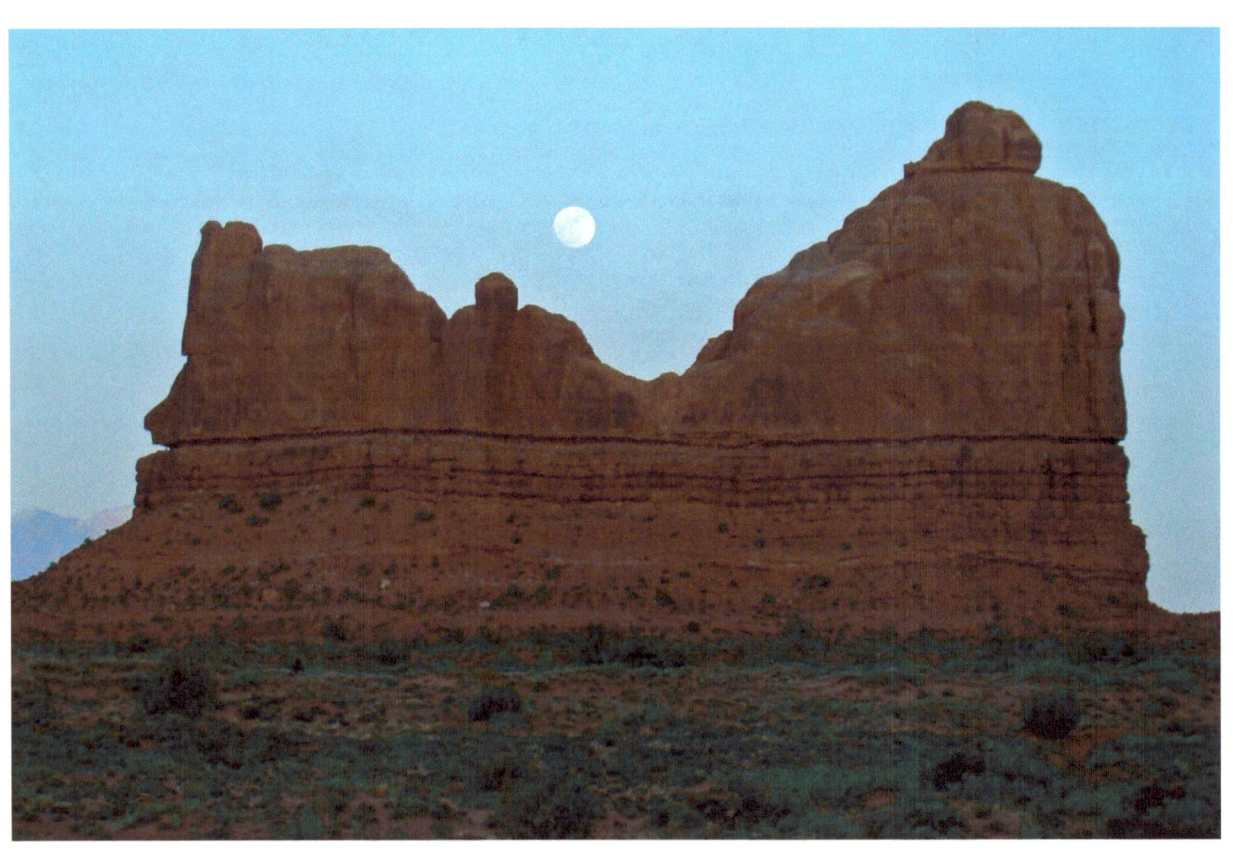

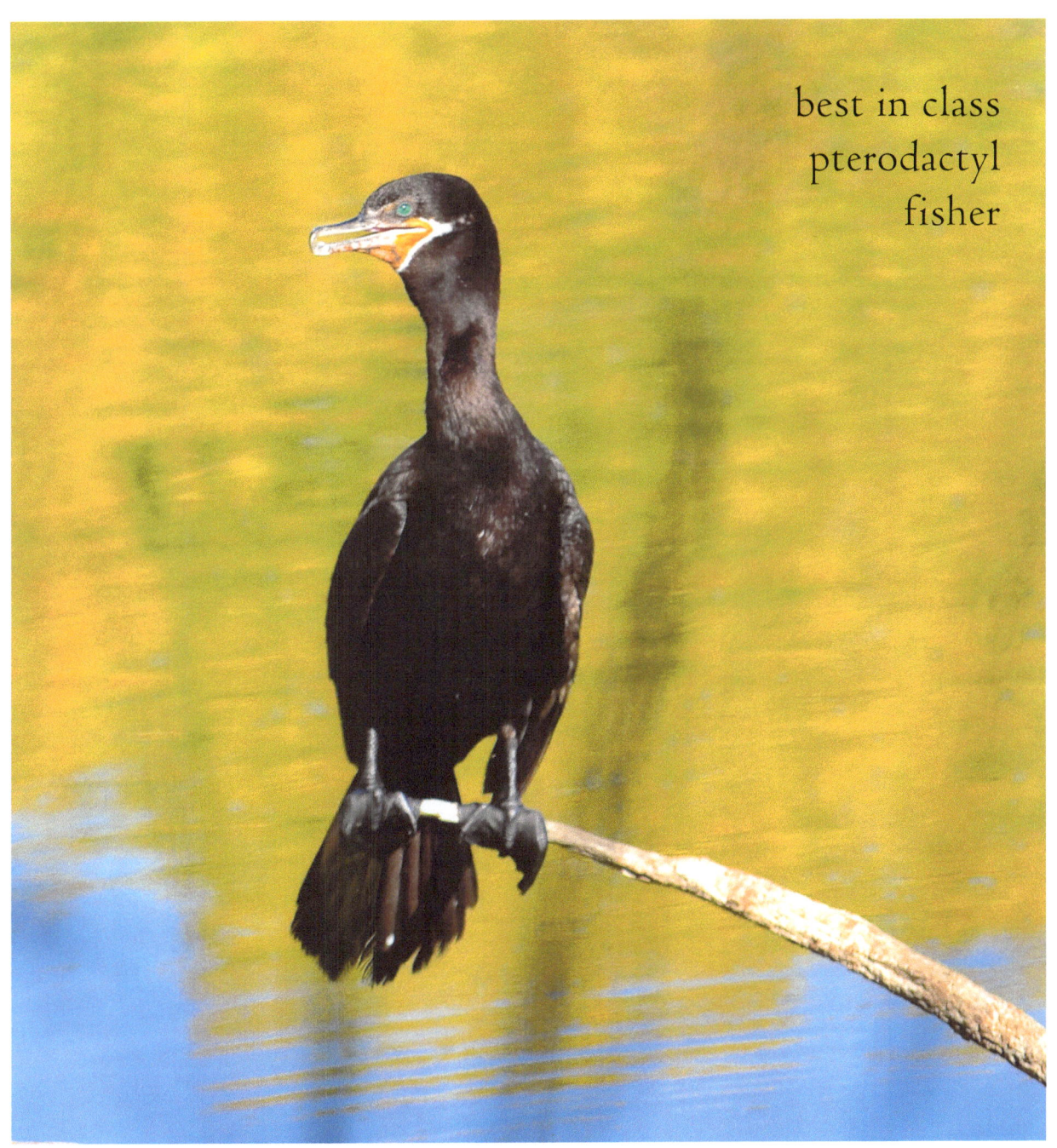

best in class
pterodactyl
fisher

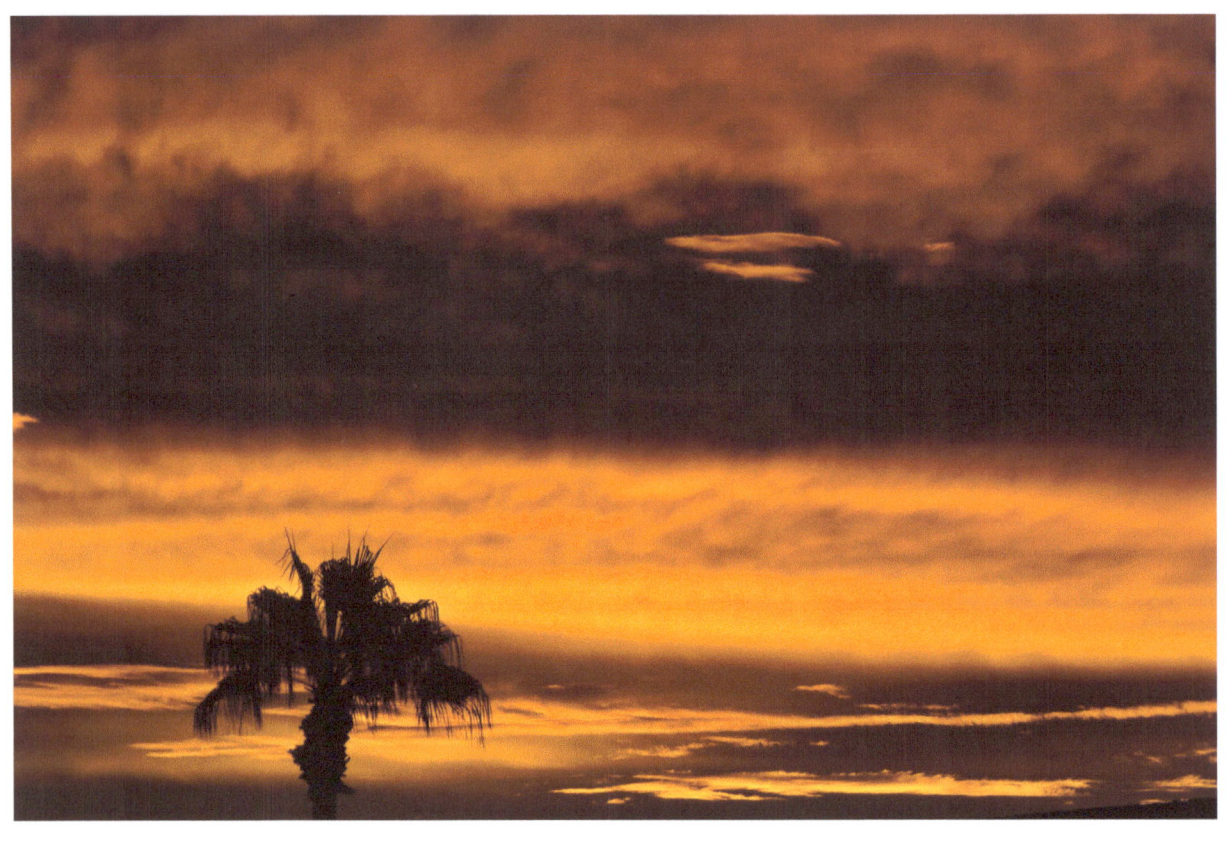

sky
to earth
Hello

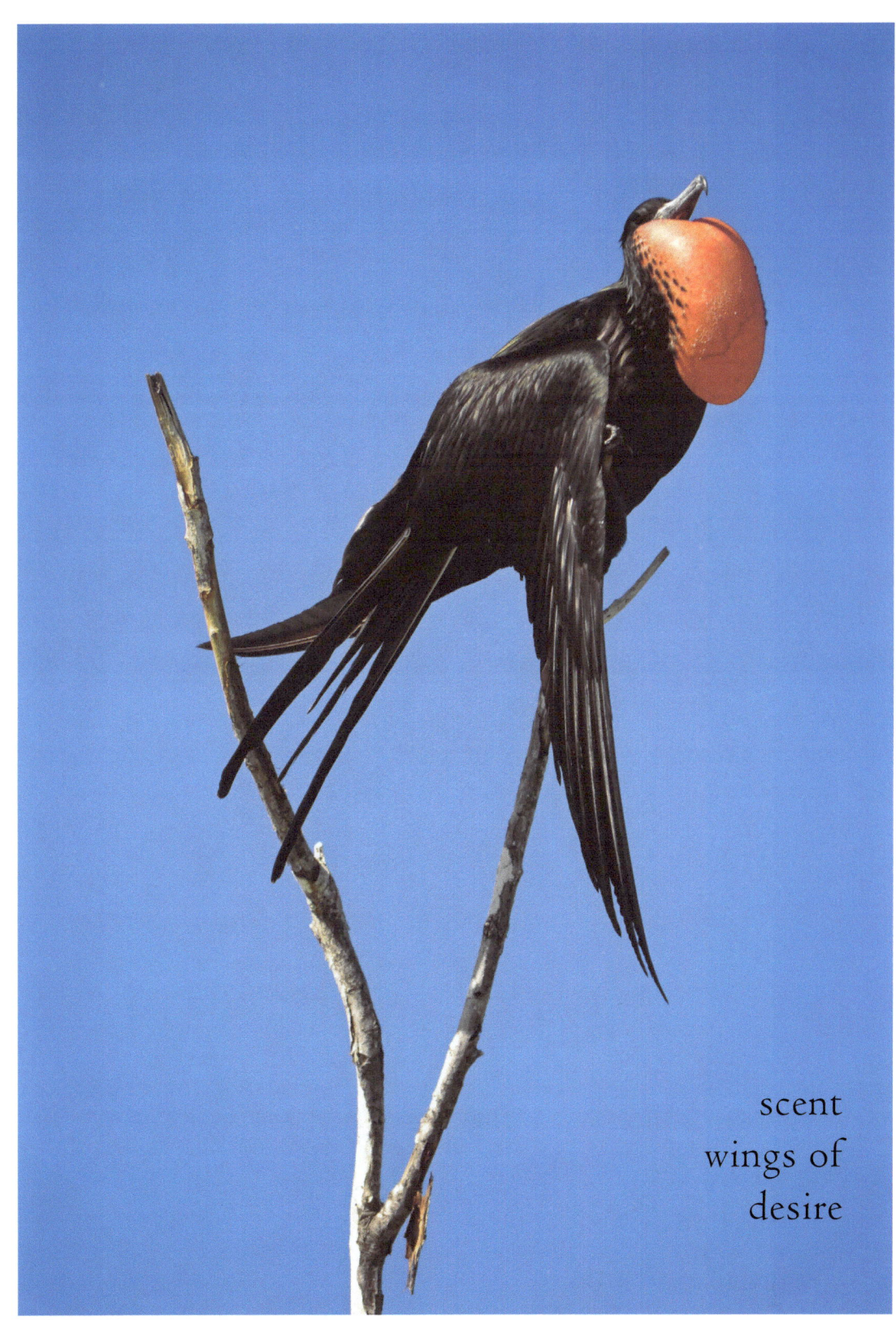

scent
wings of
desire

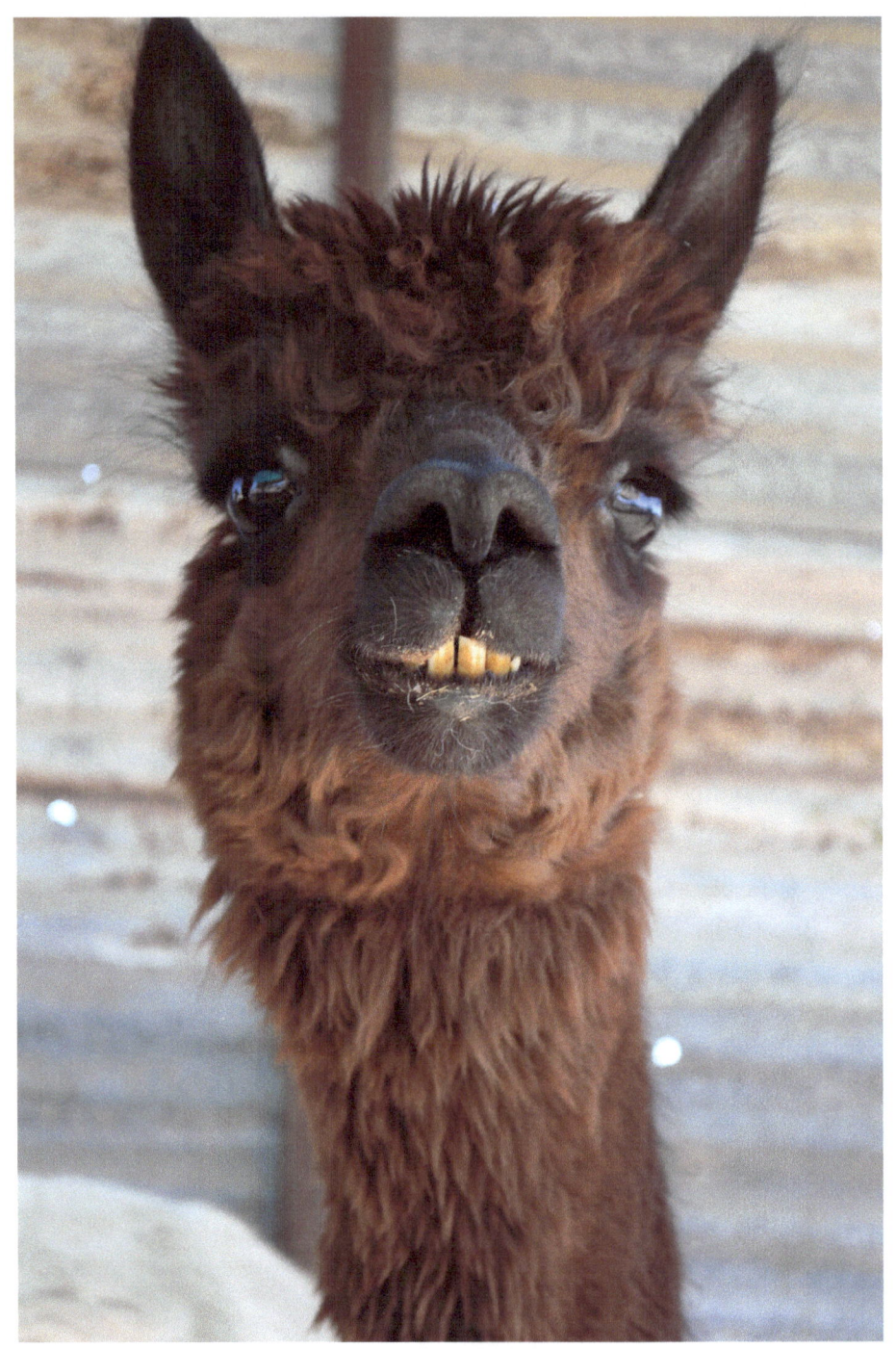

earth treasures
scrambled eggs
two-leggeds' brains

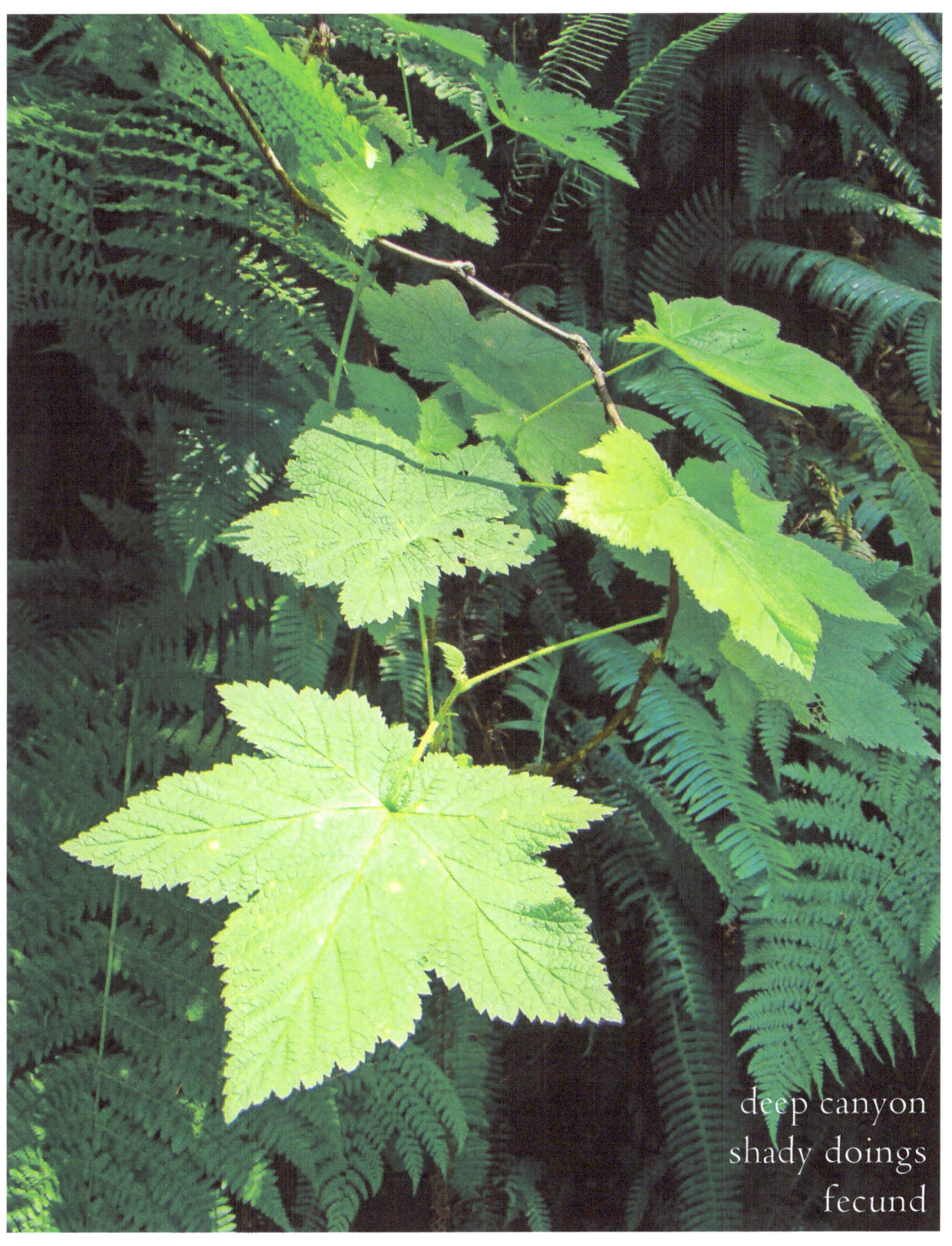

deep canyon
shady doings
fecund

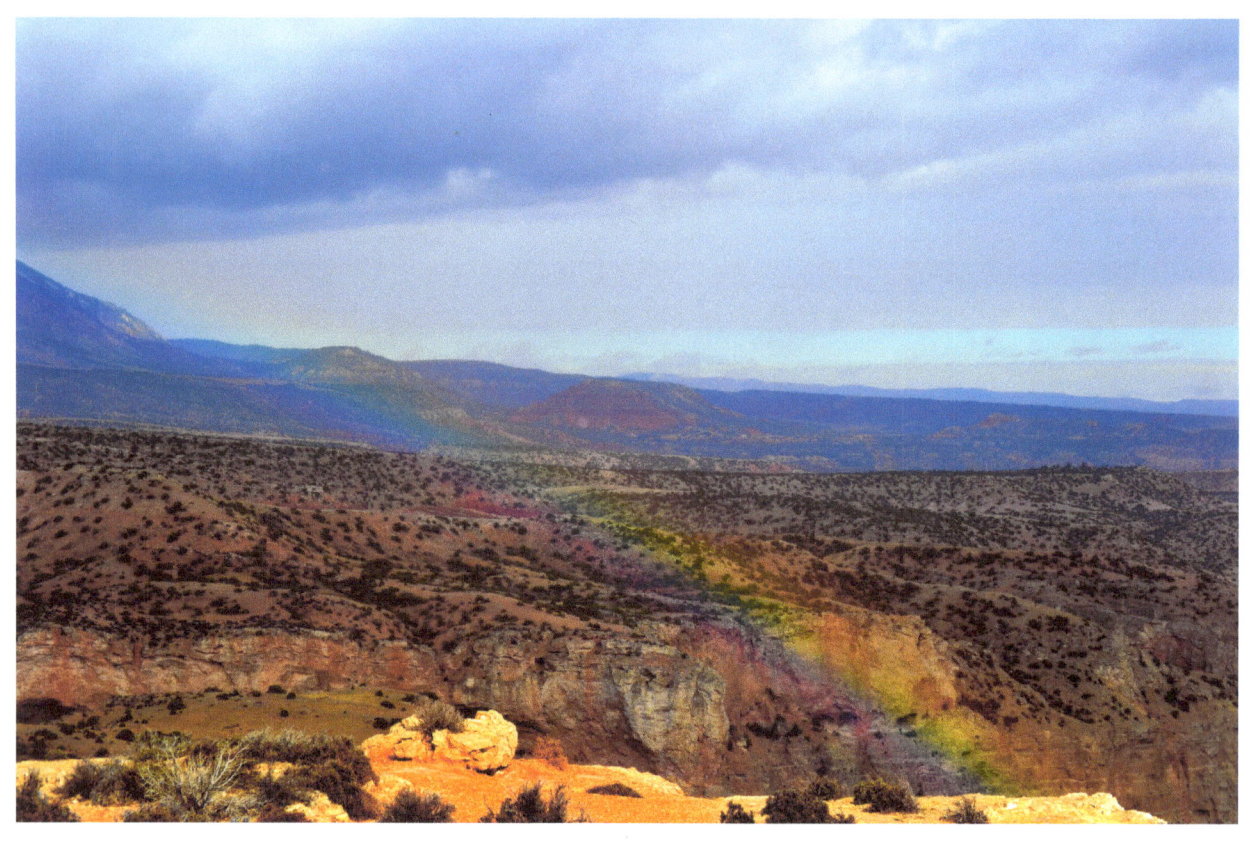

diverse
palette
high desert

sticking out
cactus spines
my neck

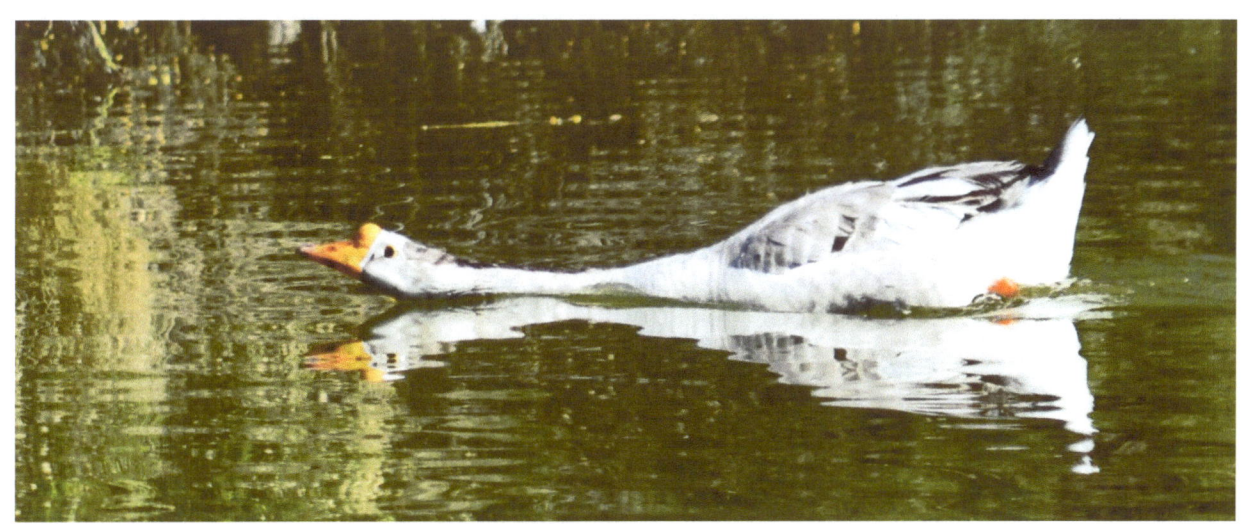

into the end zone
sprinting
to live another day

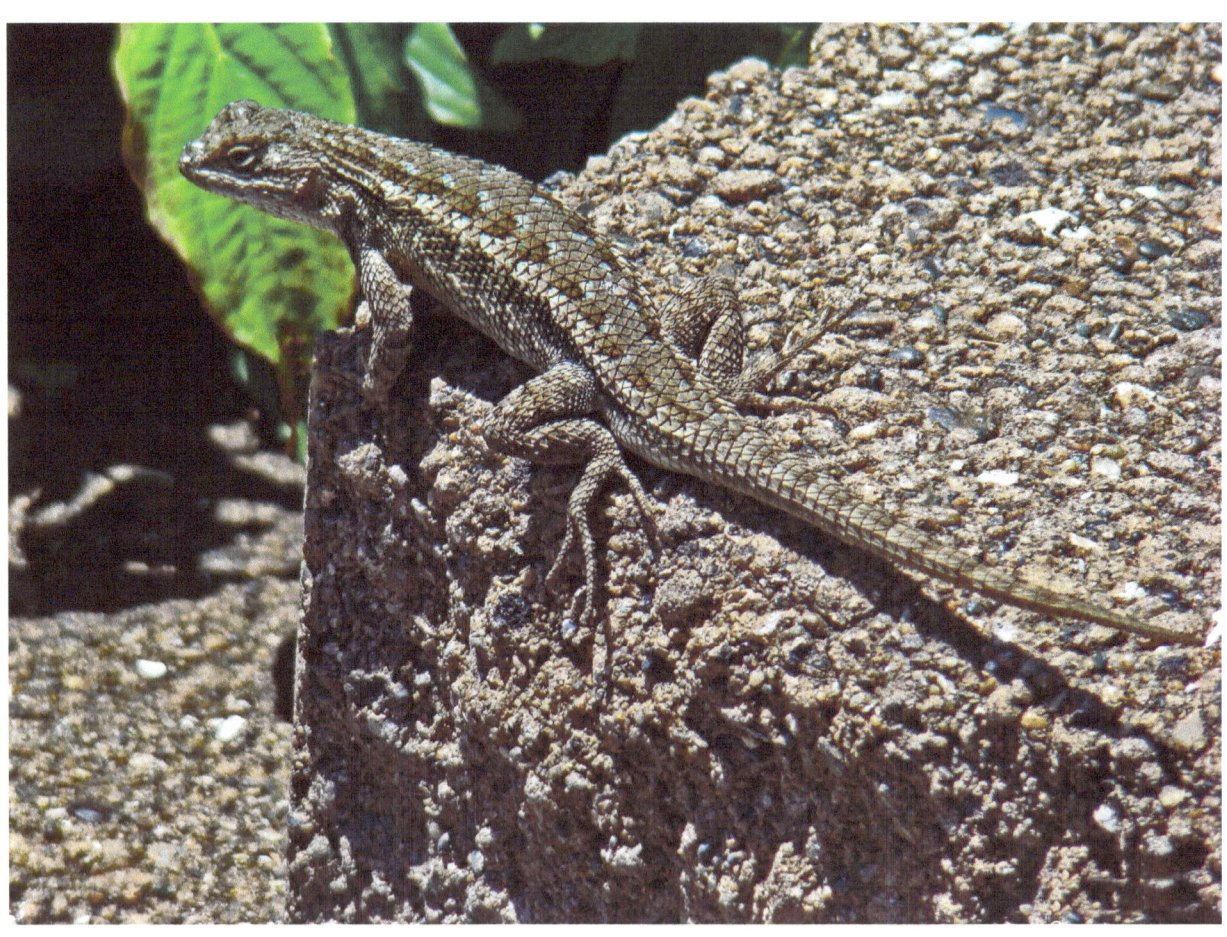

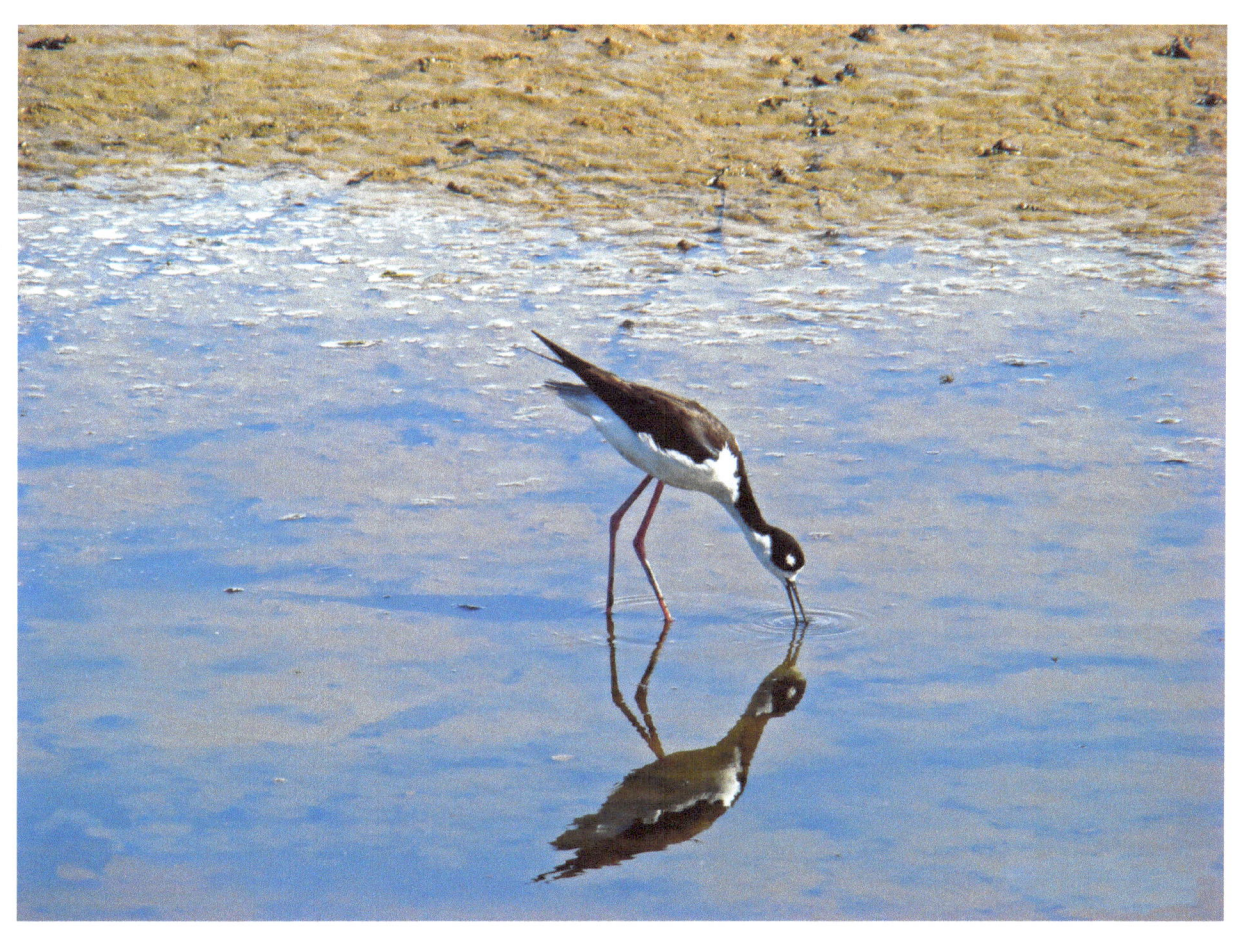

mudflats
spam in a can
sunrise

when
load
too heavy

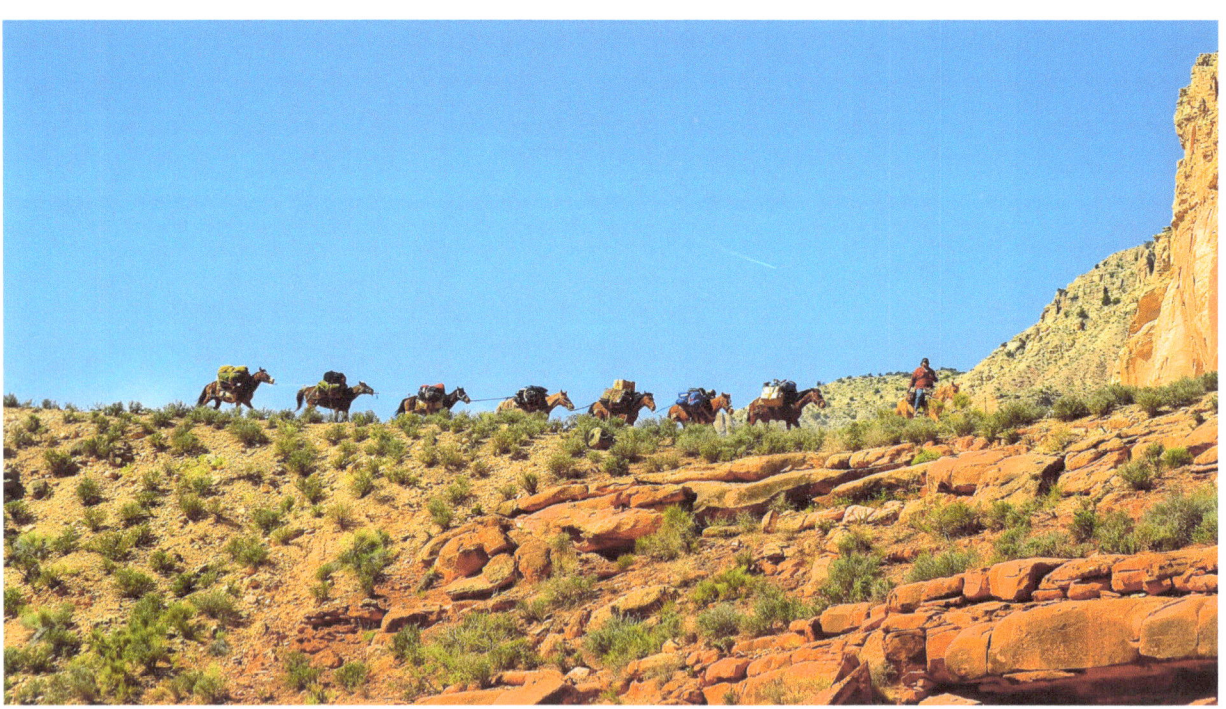

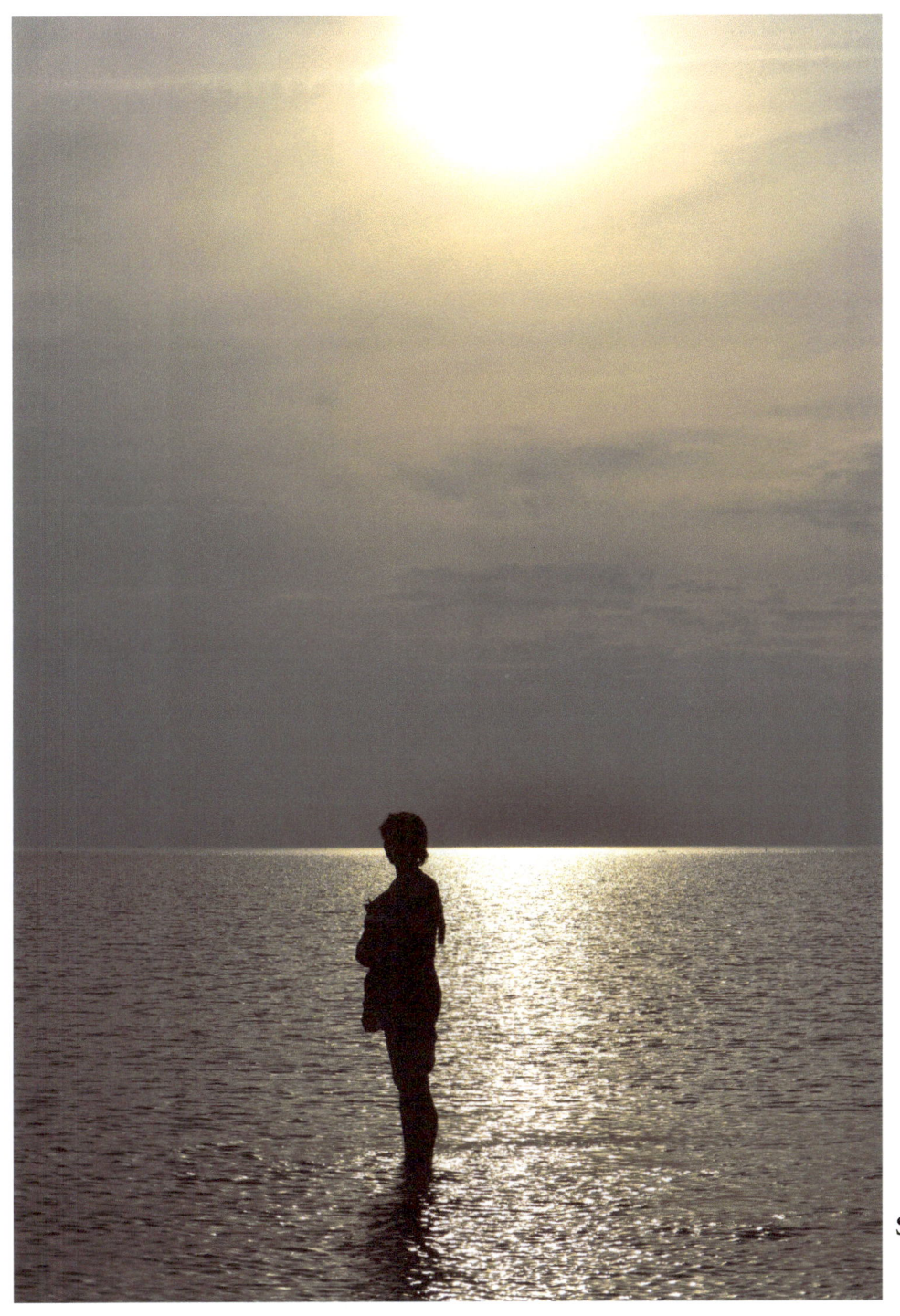

standing
tall
in the light

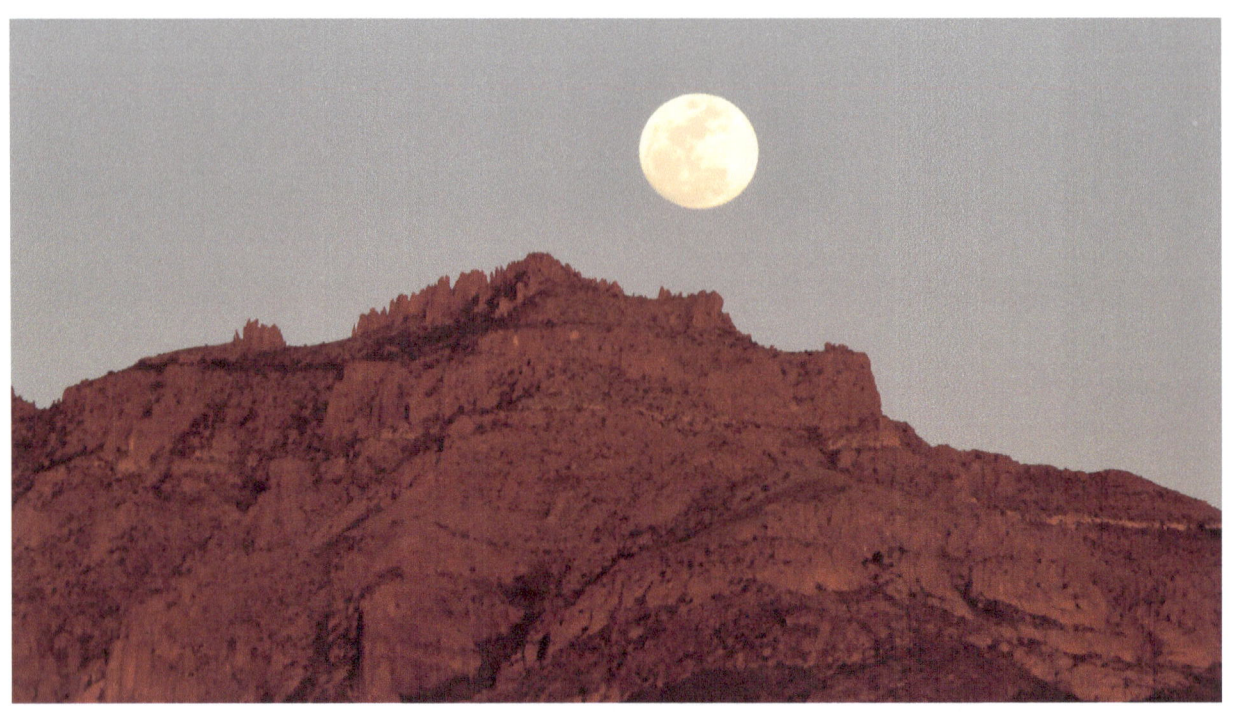

checking out
shift change
checking in

desert
monsoon
energy

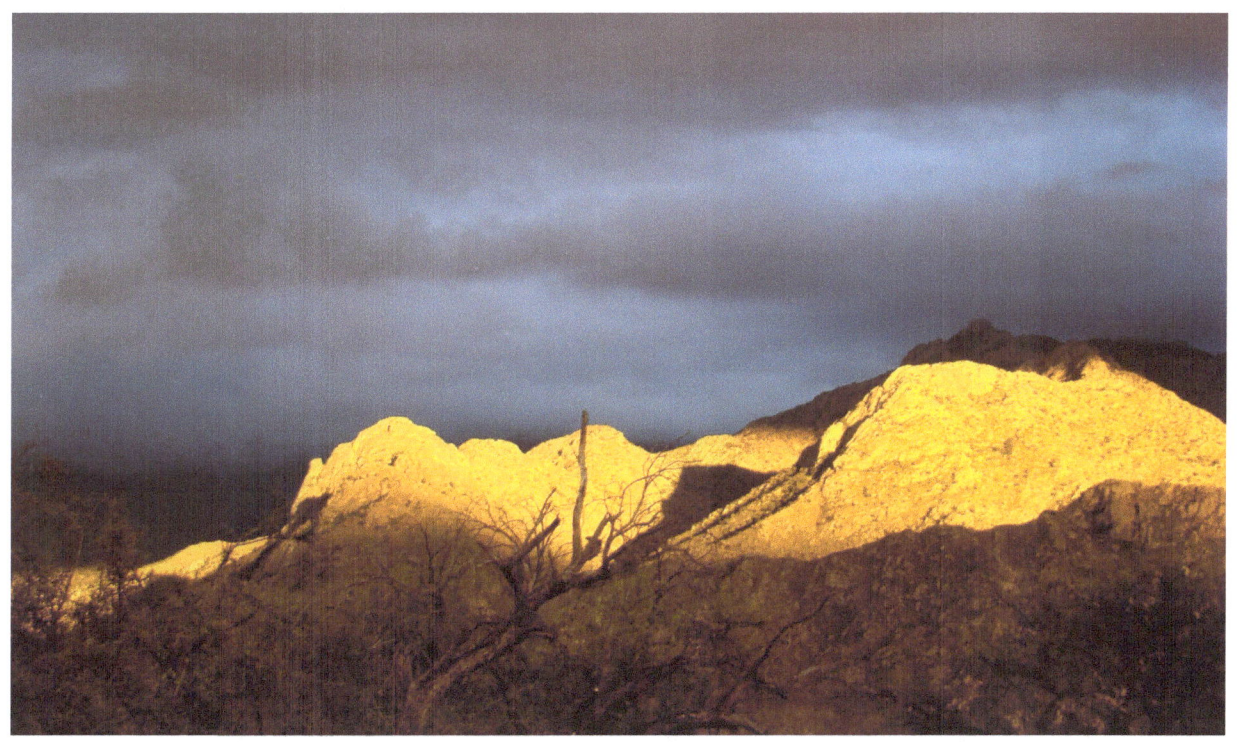

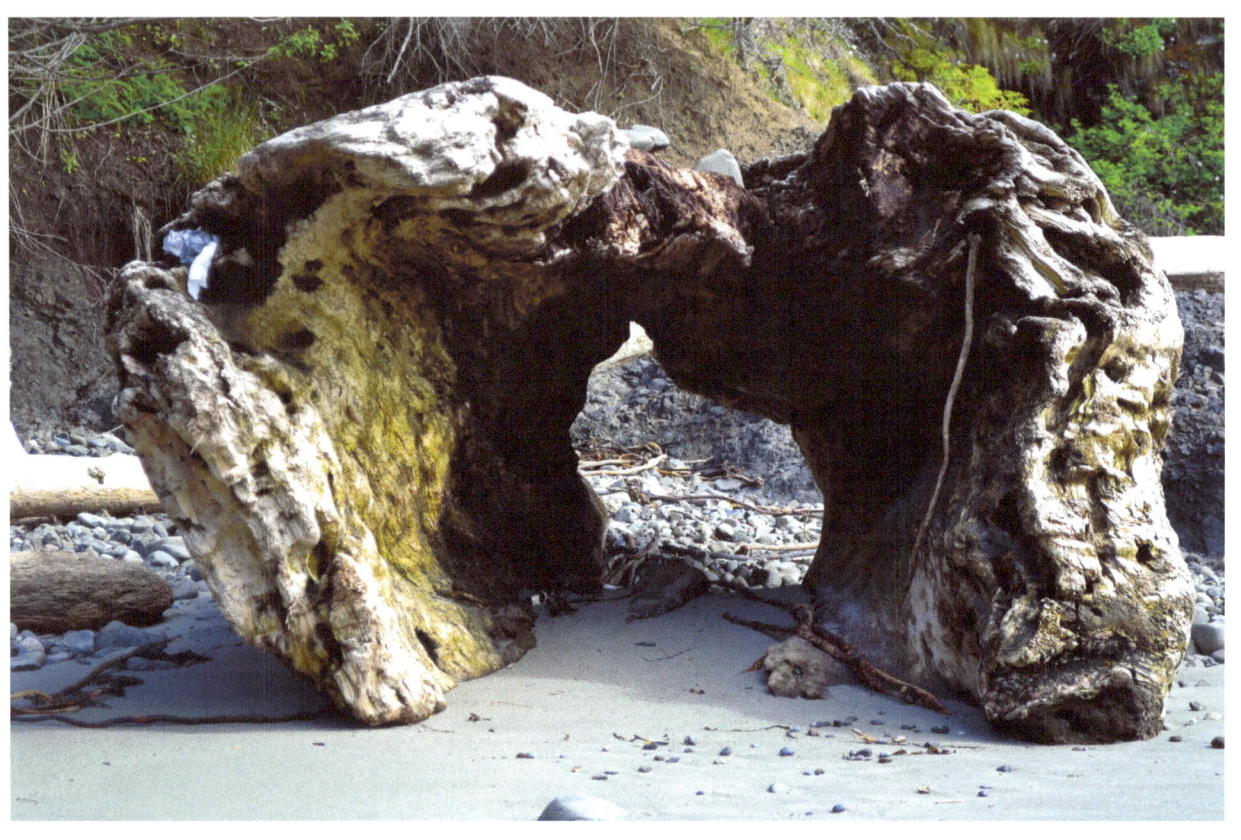

water

space

artist

sand crabs
covert
mission

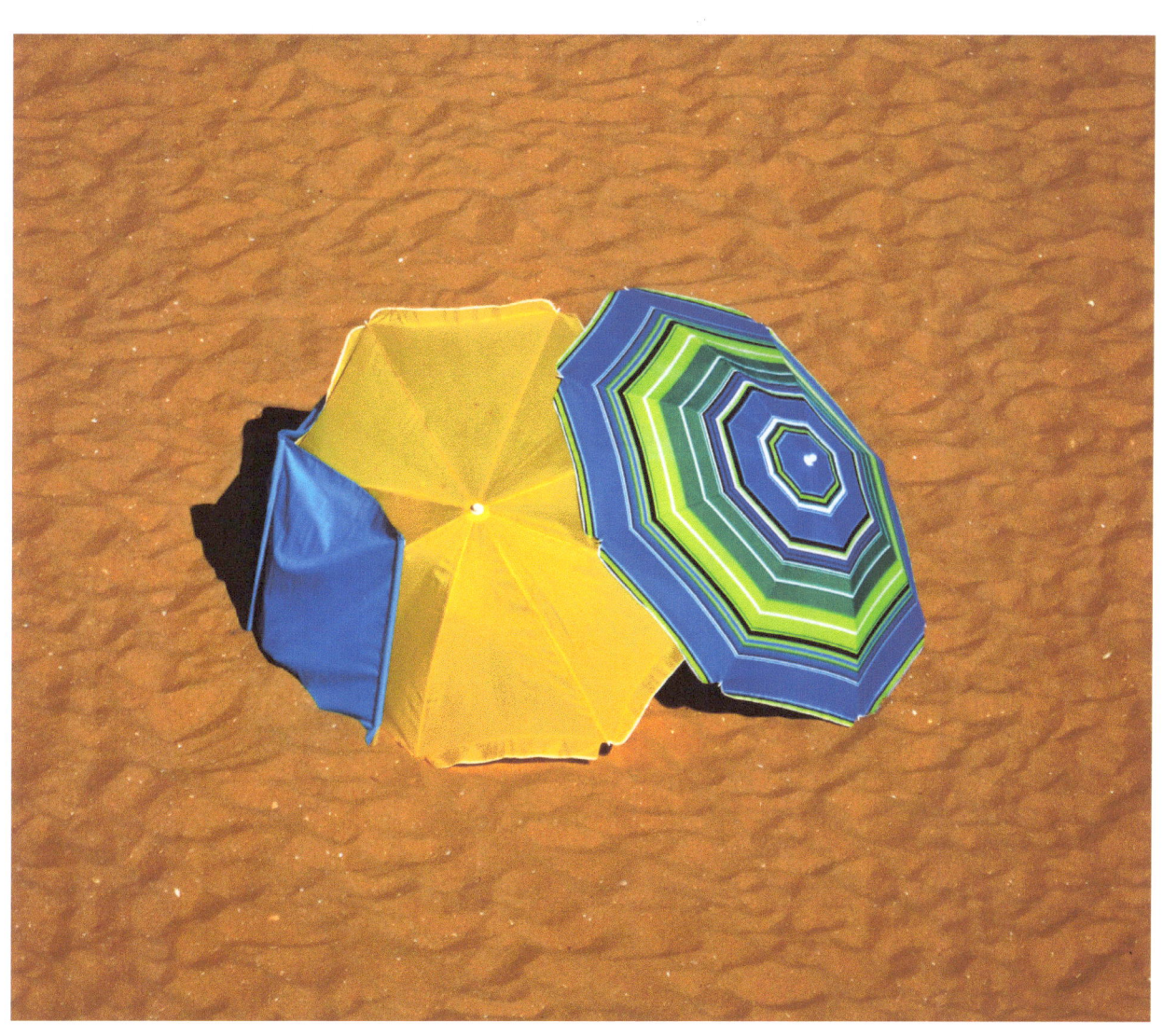

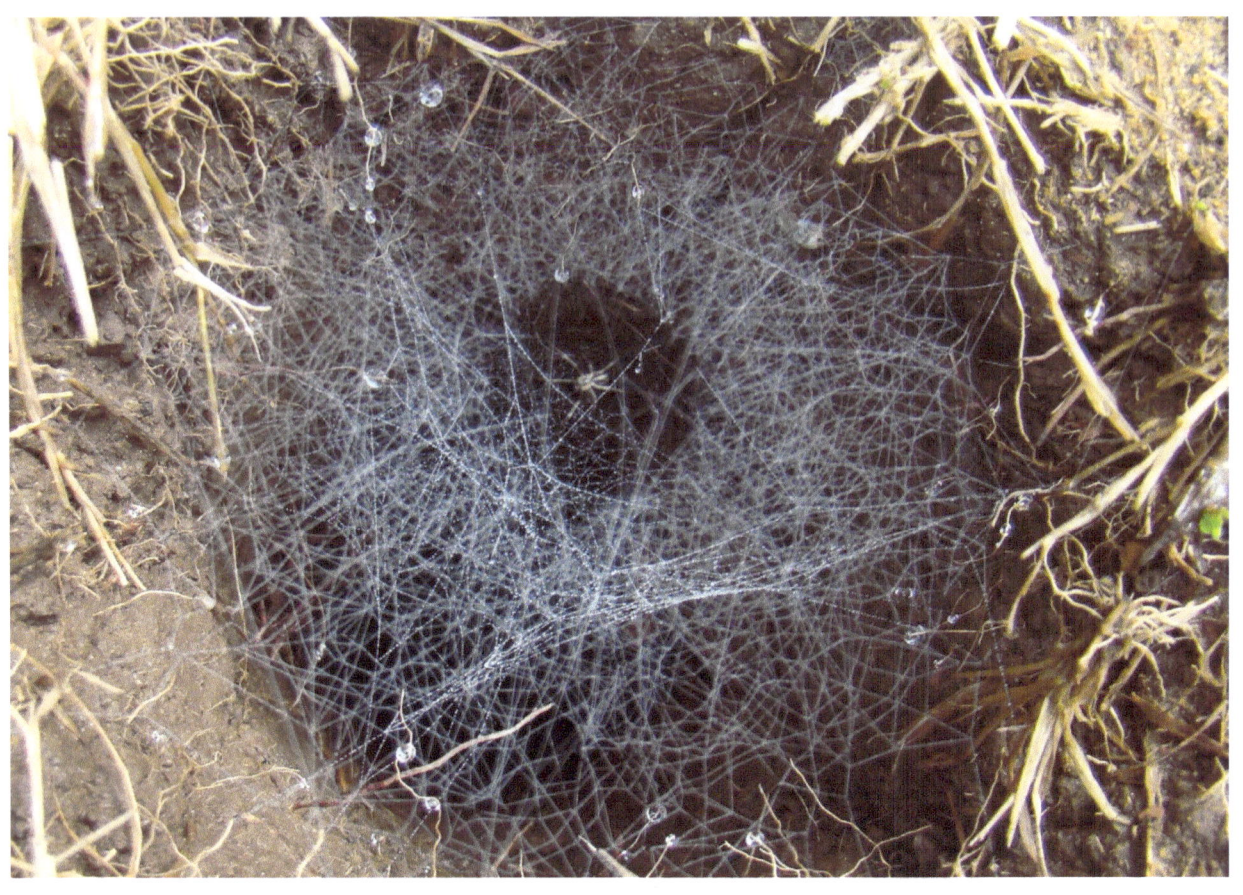

pretender
in its own web
snared

sipping
waystation
milkweed

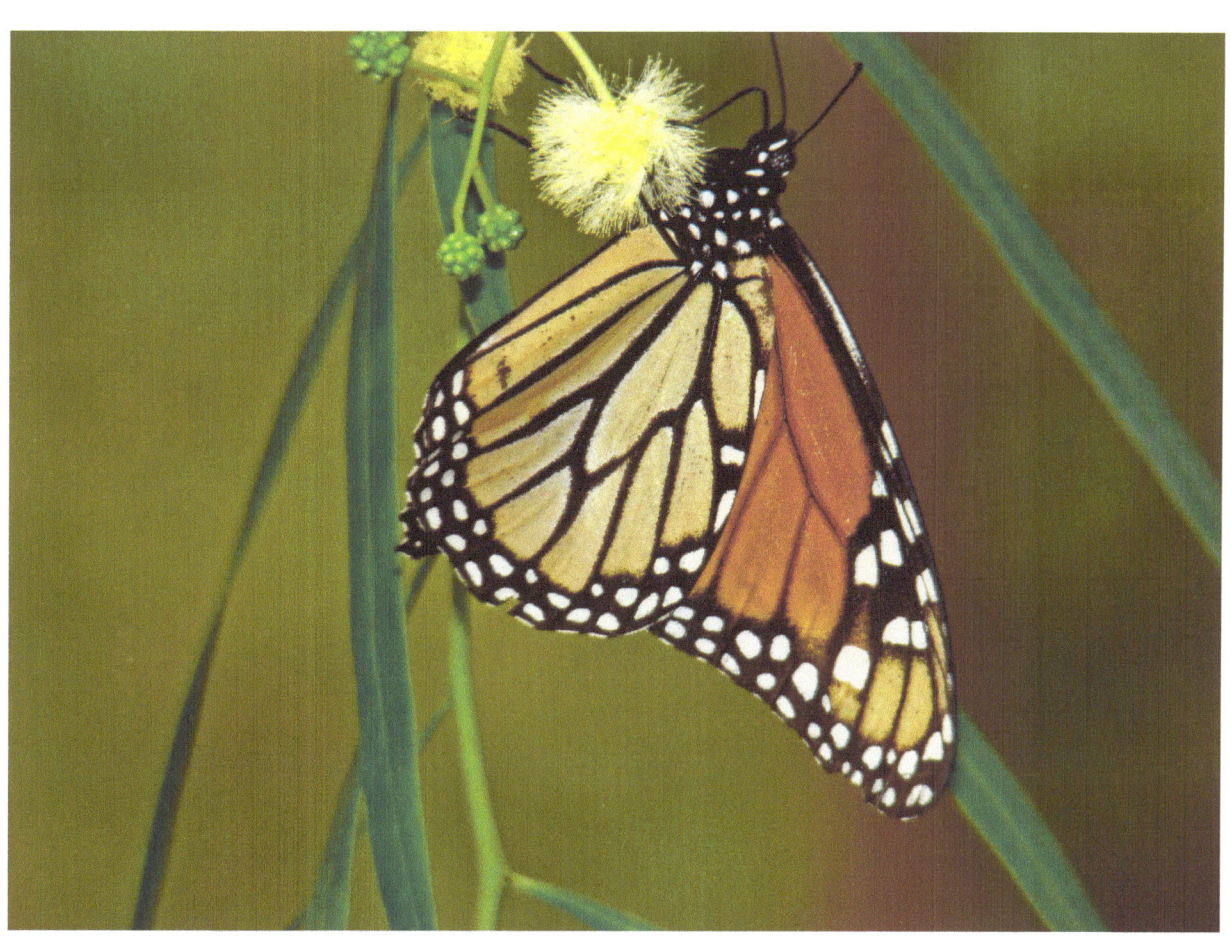

vigor
in the
cracks

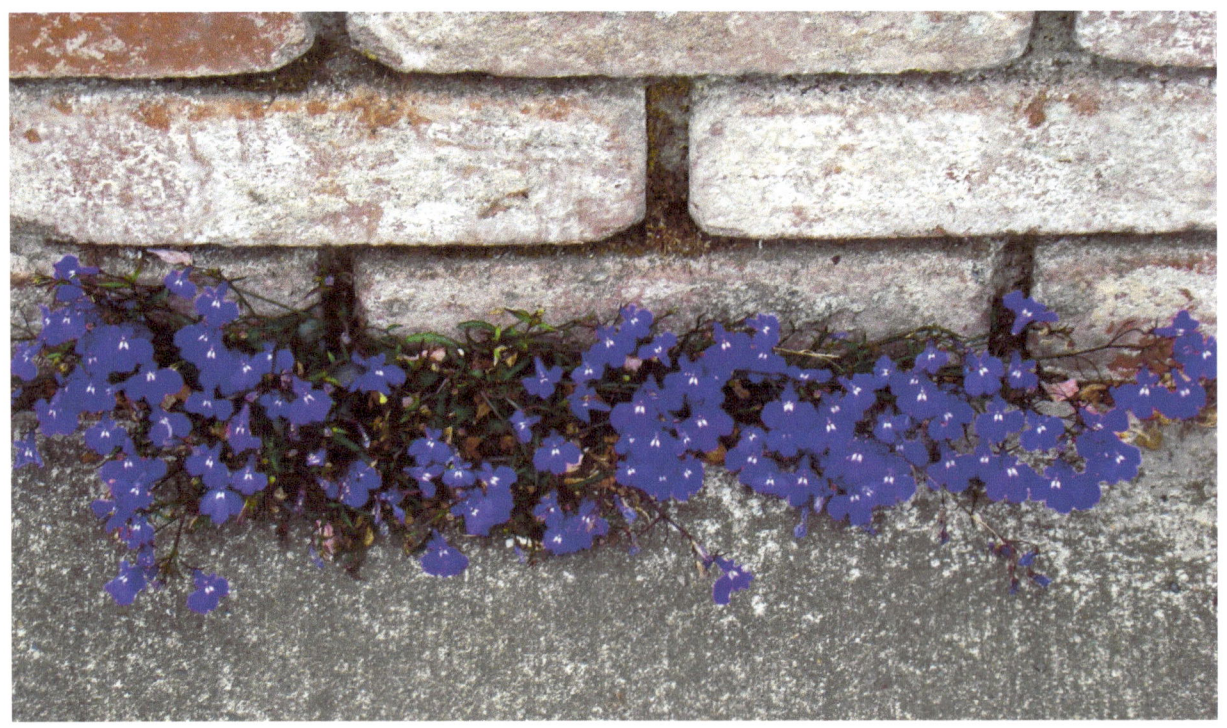

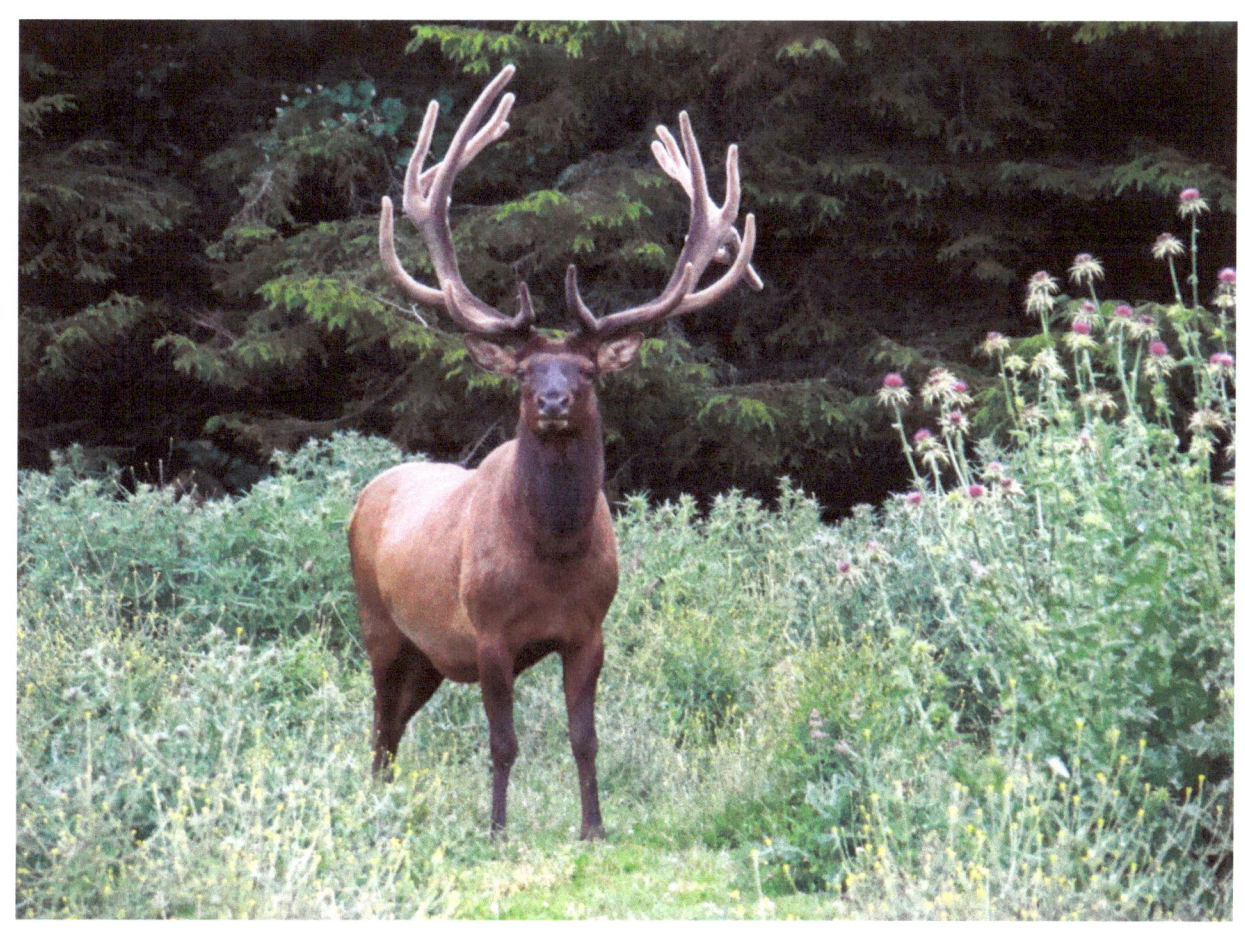

alert
grasslands
bull elk

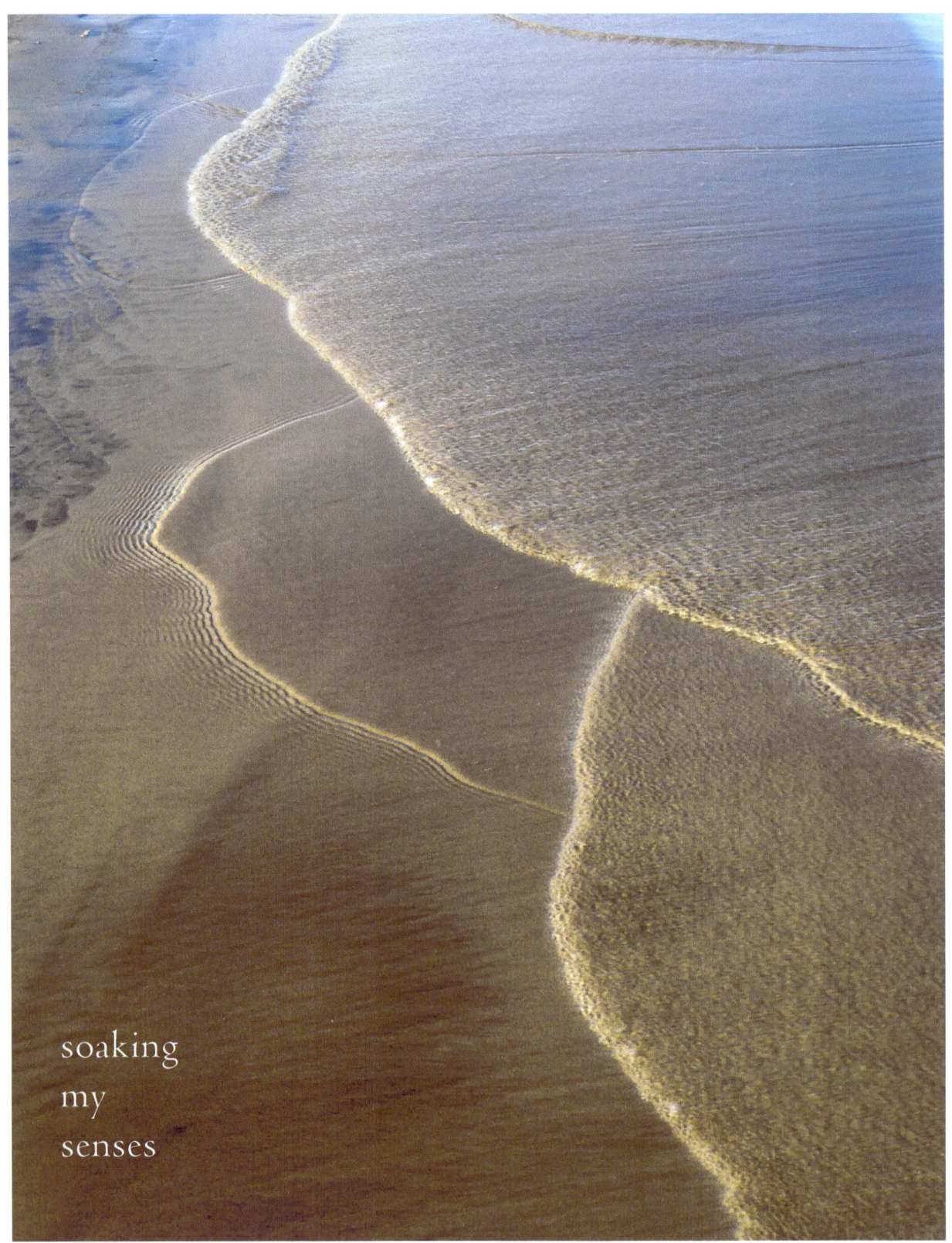
soaking my senses

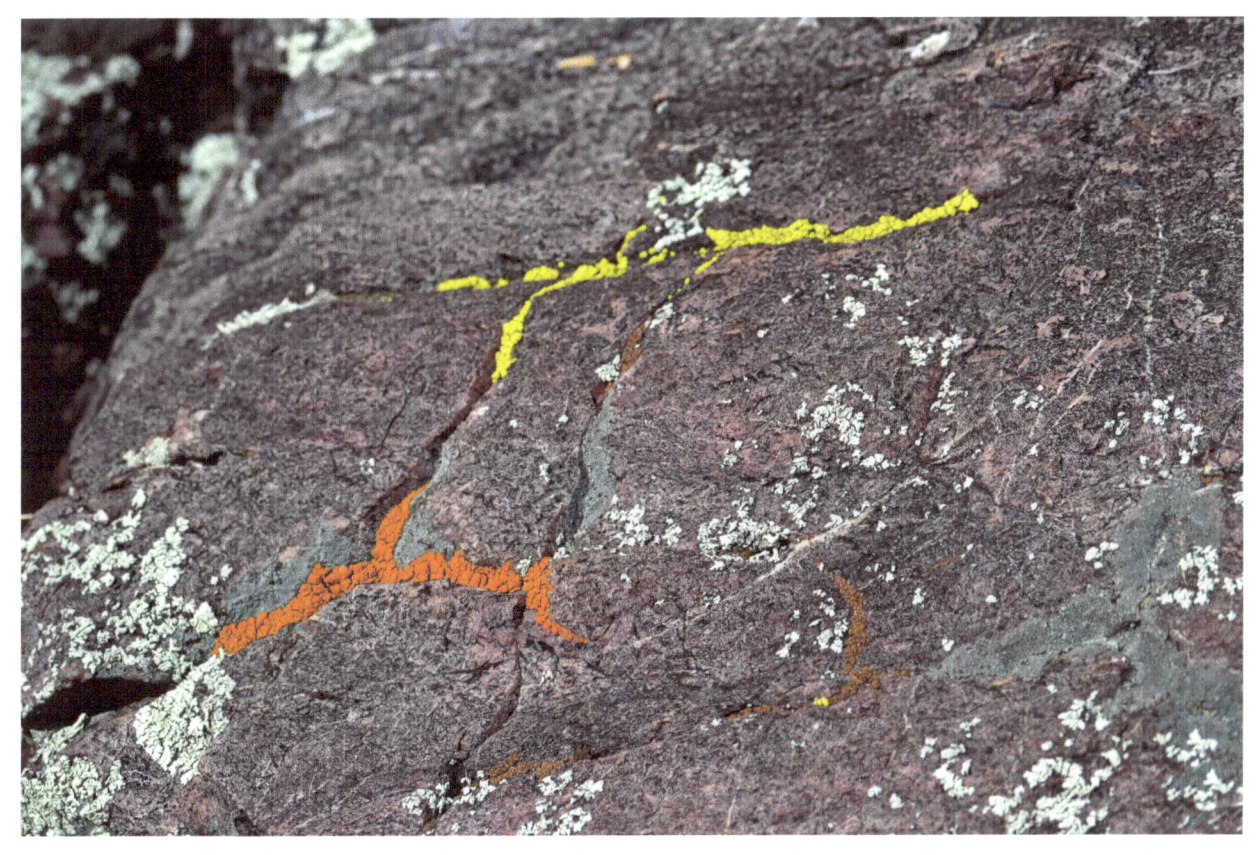

caught

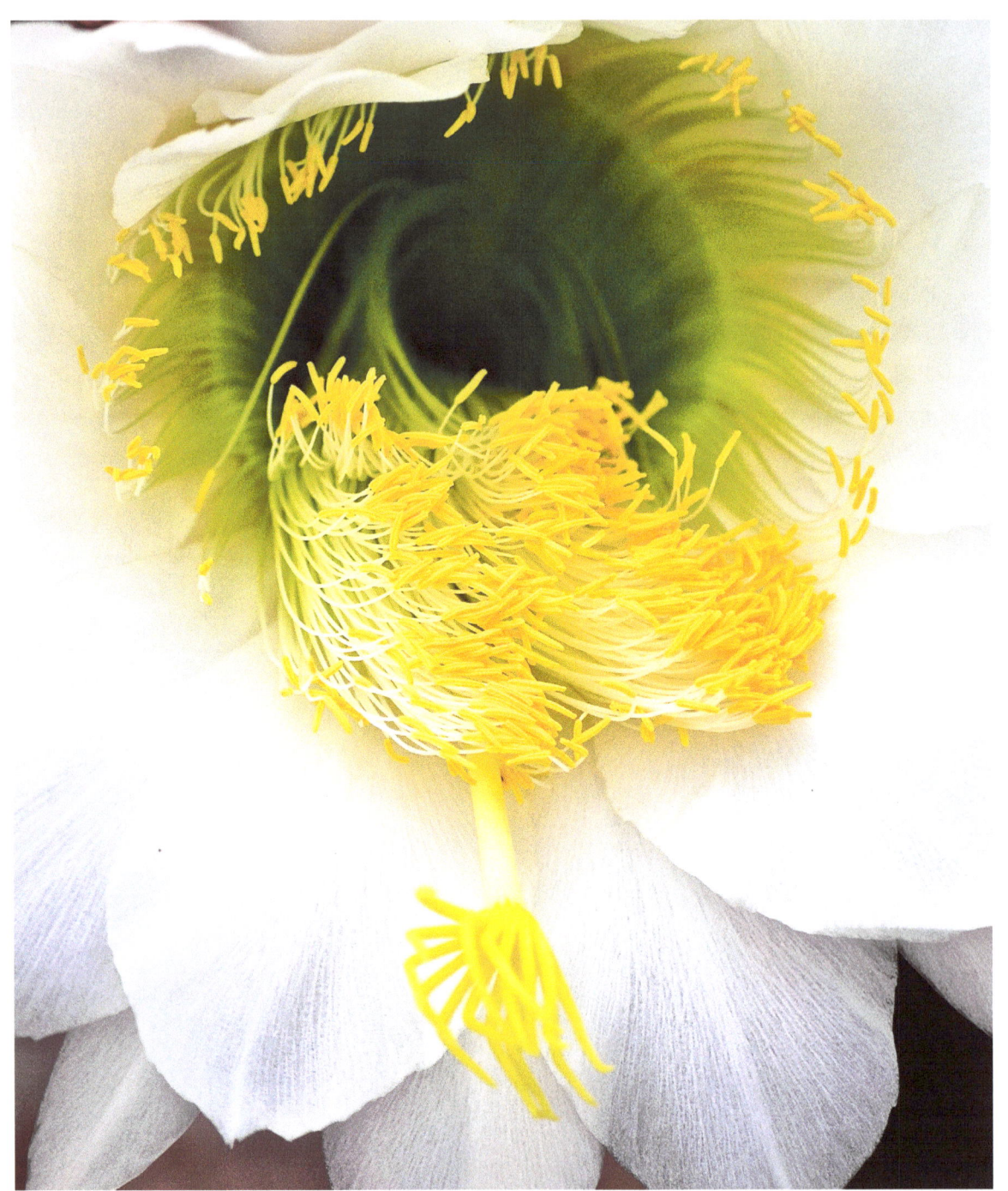

whirling
release
from within

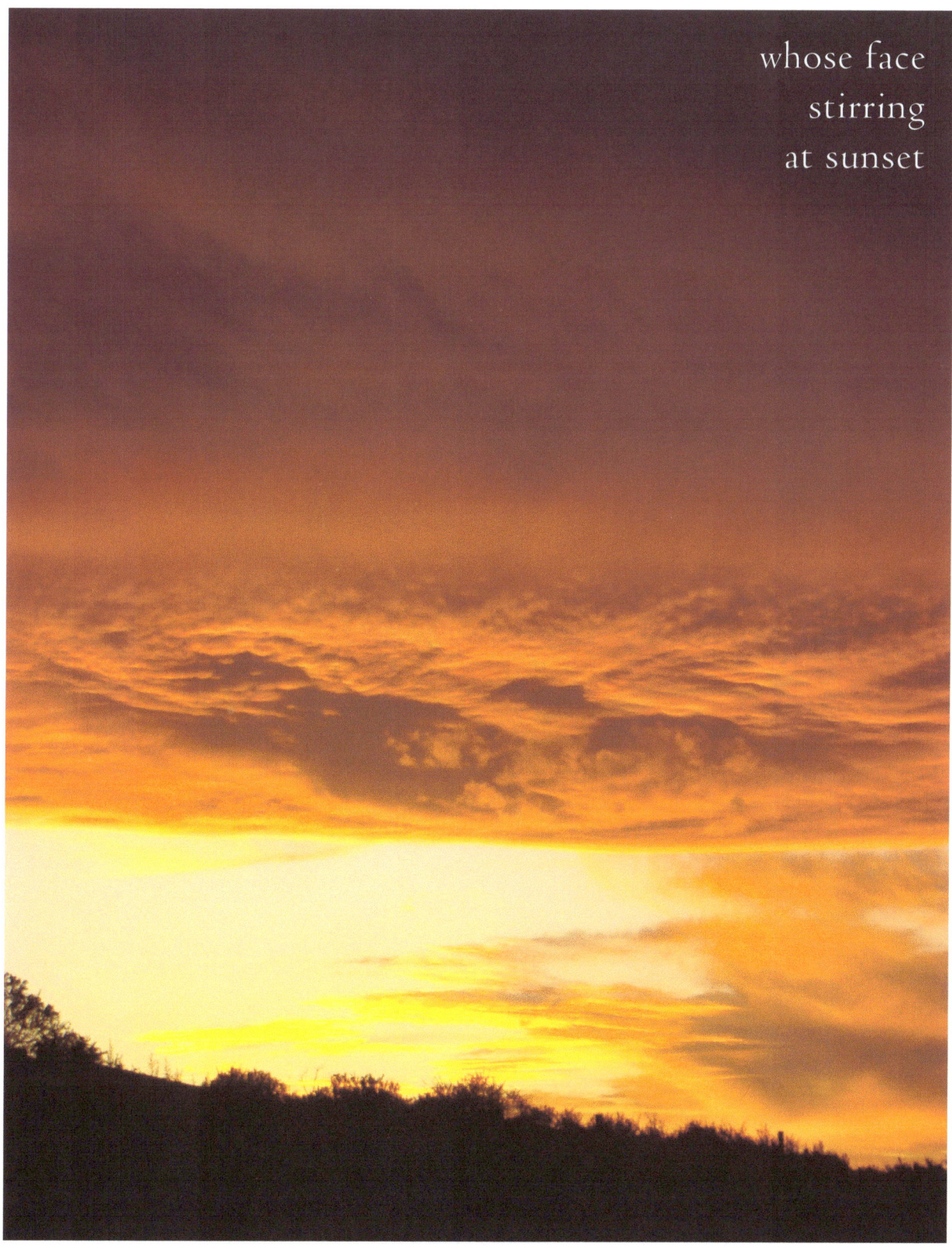

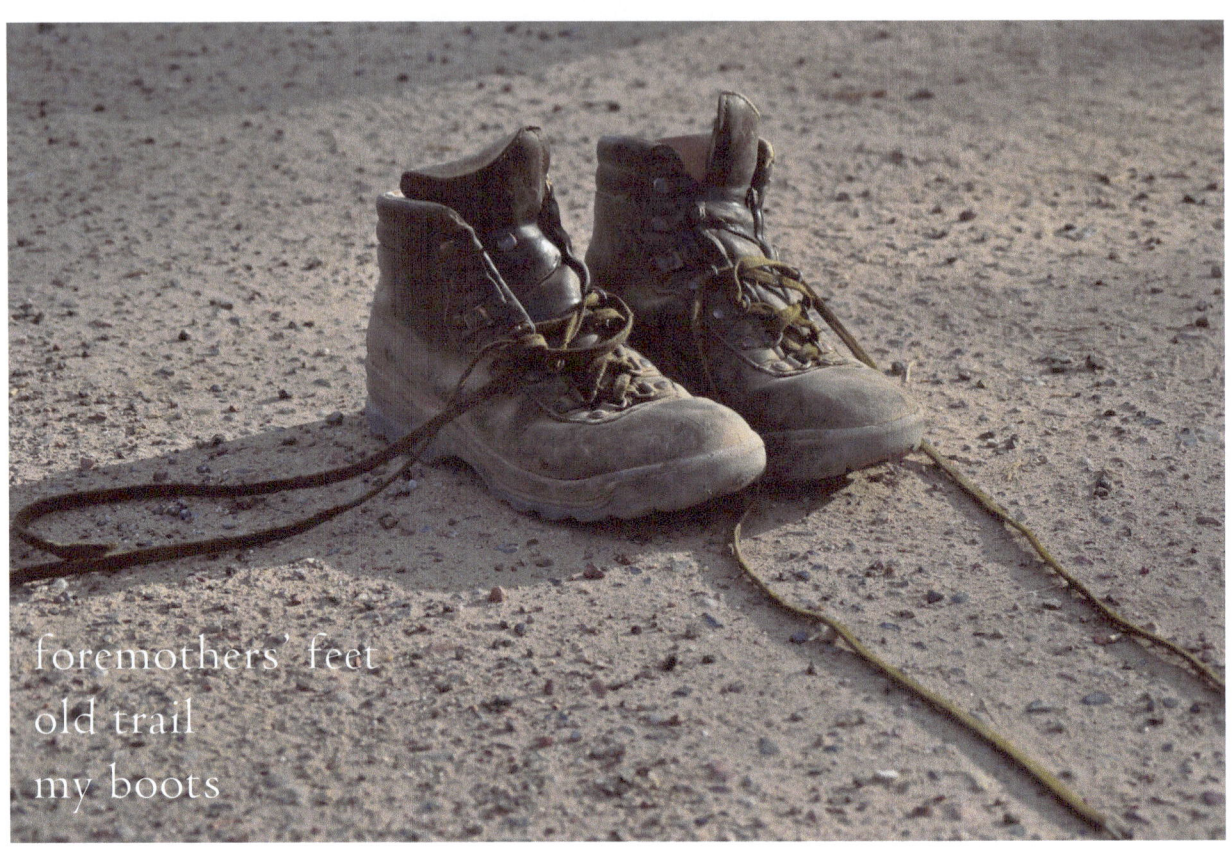

foremothers' feet
old trail
my boots

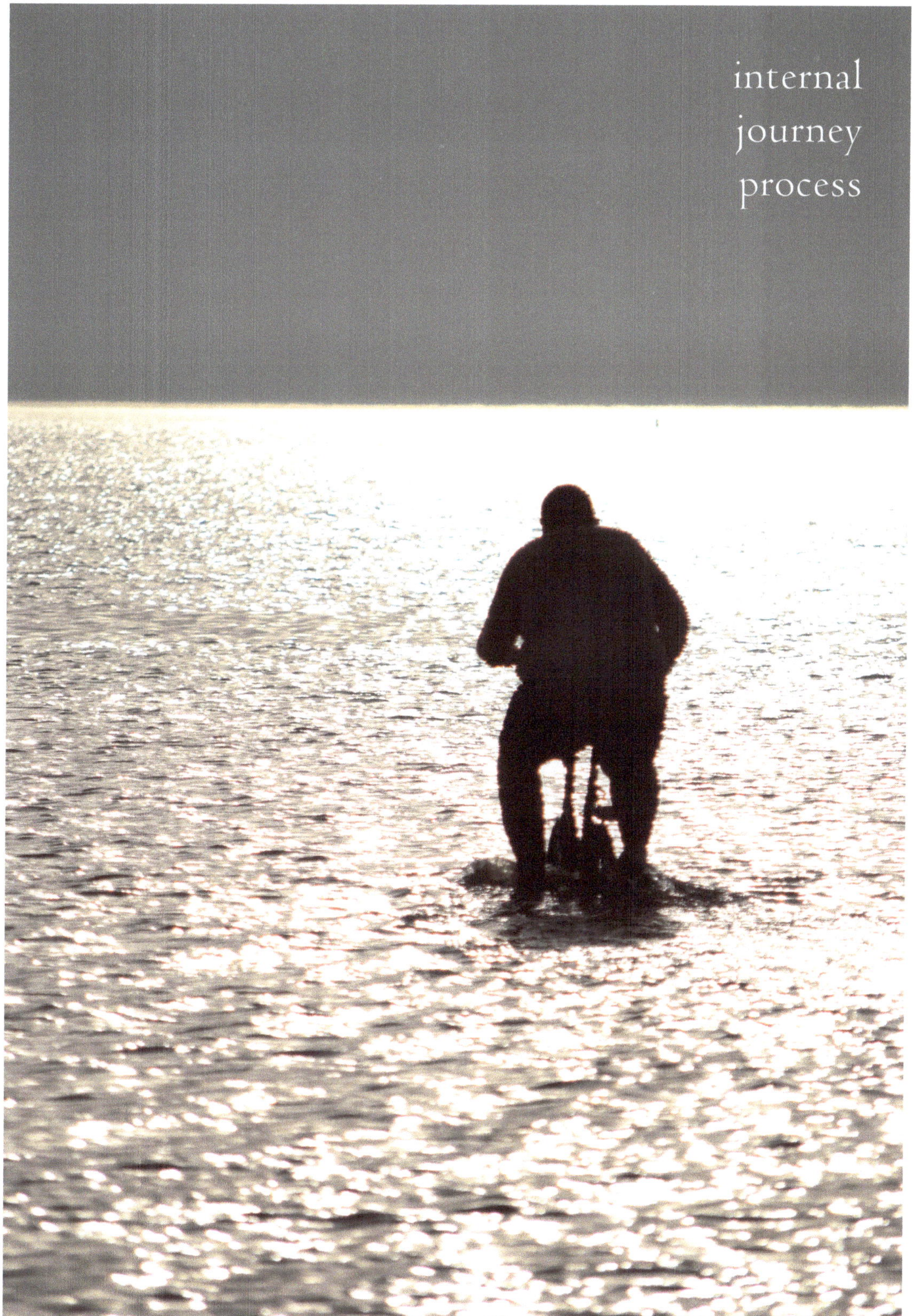

internal
journey
process

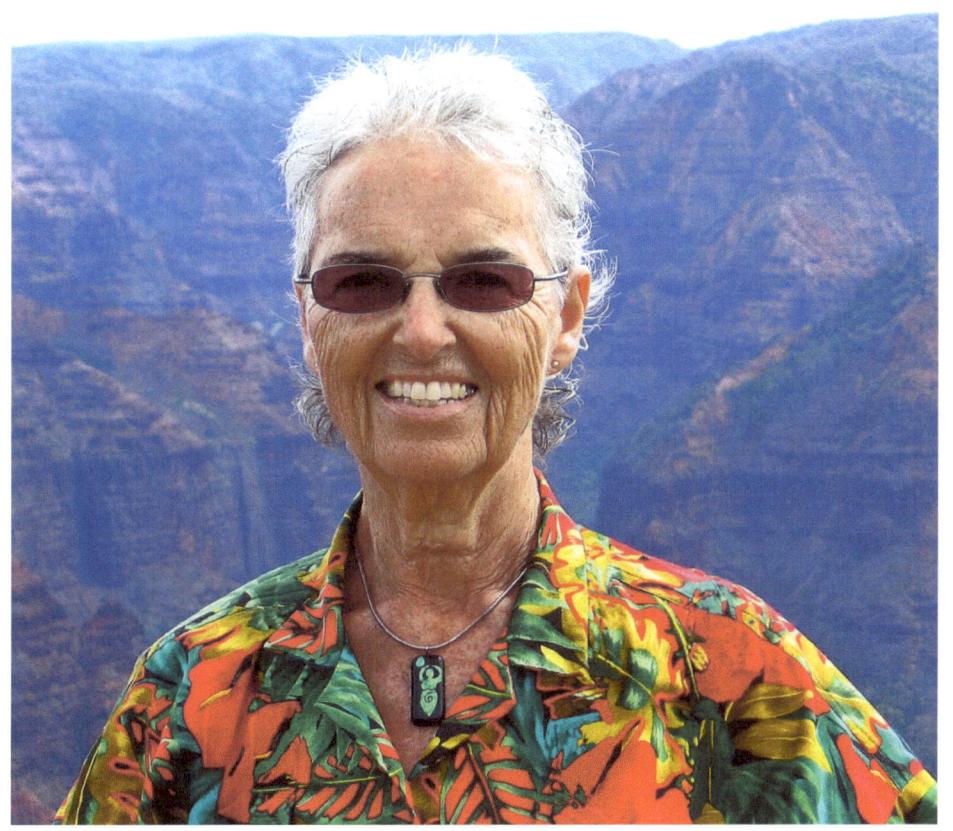

A native of Bucks County, Pennsylvania, Barbara Buck has previously published three books of classical haiku (bamboo autumn, heart of pine and sun moon sky). In this book, she stretches into a contemporary form of haiku as an accompaniment to the photographs of Janna Blok.

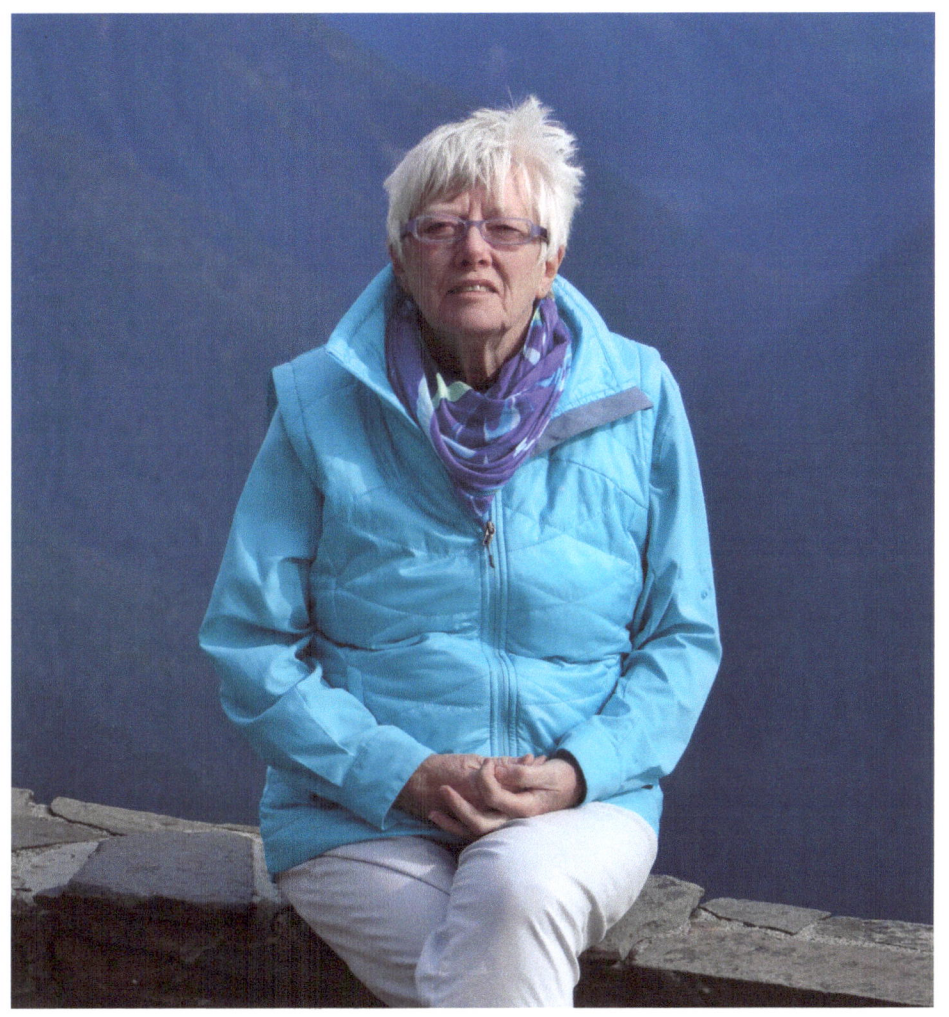

Janna Blok has been making art and teaching for over forty years. She started out as a professional potter and then evolved into a glass artist. Photography was always part of her life by taking pictures of her own work. Later on, working and traveling in different countries, she began taking pictures wherever she found the inspiration, using the light or an intriguing scene. That is how the pictures in this book came to life.

www.ingramcontent.com/pod-product-compliance
Lightning Source LLC
Chambersburg PA
CBHW051158220526
45473CB00003B/823